I0809892

IMAGES
of Sports

PROVIDENCE COLLEGE BASKETBALL
THE FRIAR LEGACY

Marvin Barnes (left) and Ernie DiGregorio are pictured during a game. Together, they were known as the Ernie D. and Marvin B. Show.

IMAGES
of Sports

PROVIDENCE COLLEGE BASKETBALL

THE FRIAR LEGACY

Richard Coren

ARCADIA
PUBLISHING

ISBN 978-0-7385-0995-2

Published by Arcadia Publishing
Charleston, South Carolina

Printed in the United States of America

Library of Congress Catalog Card Number: 2001099219

For all general information contact Arcadia Publishing at:
Telephone 843-853-2070
Fax 843-853-0044
E-mail sales@arcadiapublishing.com
For customer service and orders:
Toll-Free 1-888-313-2665

Visit us on the Internet at www.arcadiapublishing.com

The Friars began play in the 12,993-seat Providence Civic Center (now known as the Dunkin' Donuts Center) *c.* 1972. The team won its first 41 games in the building.

Contents

ACKNOWLEDGMENTS

All photographs are courtesy of Providence College unless otherwise noted. A special thanks goes to Arthur Parks, the sports information director at Providence College, and Jane Jackson, the director of archives at Providence College. All photographs later than 1973 were taken by Tom Maguire unless otherwise noted. A special thanks goes to Tom for the use of his excellent images. A thank-you also goes to current school president Rev. Philip A. Smith, O.P., for giving the basketball program the attention it needs to remain competitive and healthy. Finally, thanks go to Gregg Burke for allowing me to introduce myself 12 years ago.

This book is dedicated to my parents, who are Providence College fans through and through and, more importantly, my biggest fans.

INTRODUCTION

On February 14, 1956, a little-used substitute named Gordie Holmes took an inbounds pass near the end of overtime and launched a 45-foot prayer that not only stunned Notre Dame but also launched the modern era of Providence College basketball.

Over the past 45 years, Friar basketball has captured the imagination of sports fans in Rhode Island and throughout New England. From humble beginnings, the small Dominican school on Smith Hill in Providence has produced a David and Goliath story.

The legend persists—tiny Providence College takes on and beats the big boys of college basketball. It is the story of a program that was run on a shoestring budget in the 1950s and 1960s and rose up out of nowhere to pull upset after upset. The basketball program grew to dominate college basketball in New England. Providence College has had more postseason tournament games and victories, more 20-win seasons, more All-Americans, and more players in the pros than any school in the region.

Prior to 1956, the college had enjoyed tremendous success in basketball, especially in the late 1920s and the 1930s. A latecomer to the sport, the Friars were the top team in New England by their third year of competition. They were the dominant program in the region over a 10-year period that extended through the late 1930s. At this time, however, despite the team's success, basketball ranked only third in importance among sports on campus, behind baseball and football.

After World War II, basketball at the college was almost an afterthought. A small school playing small-college-caliber basketball, Providence might have been destined to become a Division II program except for the vision of leaders on campus, such as school president Fr. Robert Slavin and athletic director Fr. Aloysius Begley. Looking ahead at the possibility of a small Catholic school competing in big-time college basketball, these leaders fought to upgrade the program. Alumni Hall was built and Joe Mullaney was hired as coach. With Gordi Holmes's shot, Friar basketball was about to awaken from a 15-year slumber.

By 1960, the Friars were once again established as New England's top program, and a growing legion of fans thrilled to Chris Clark's calls of heart-stopping wins, as "When the Saints Come Marching In" hearkened the arrival of another Friar triumph. The team entered the National Invitation Tournament (NIT) on a yearly basis. Rhode Islanders swarmed Madison Square Garden, and the tournament was won. Tens of thousands of adoring fans were present to welcome their heroes home, and the team had a firm hold on the hearts of the region's college basketball enthusiasts.

The move to the Providence Civic Center in 1972 gave thousands of fans their first opportunity to see the team in person, and the Friars responded by capturing a new generation of fans with an NCAA Final Four team. Improbable success followed Providence College throughout the 1970s as the underdog Friars continued to knock off the big teams like top-ranked University of Michigan, University of North Carolina, and University of Louisville.

The parade of superstar players seemed unending: from Wilkens to DiGregorio, from Walker to Barnes, and from Thompson to Hassett. All were overseen by Joe Mullaney and Dave Gavitt, coaching geniuses. By the late 1970s, Providence College was firmly established as the capital of New England college basketball.

In 1980, after 52 seasons as an independent, the college made the move to the Big East Conference (a league it helped establish). This transition seemed to put a halt to the team's success. Forced to compete against bigger schools with more revenue, Providence College struggled for six years, and many wondered whether the team's future might not be in Division II after all.

In 1985, Rick Pitino entered the picture and injected new life into the program. Two years later, the team captured the attention of college basketball fans everywhere with a rags-to-riches season that culminated with a second NCAA Final Four appearance. Pitino showed Friar fans and school officials that it was possible for a smaller school to compete in this day and age.

Today, as Providence College celebrates its 75th season of basketball, the Friars' long and storied tradition is firmly established as one of the very best in college basketball history. The team's fans eagerly await each new chapter. The small Catholic school on Smith Hill continues to reap the benefits that the basketball program has wrought. As Father Slavin remarked in 1960, "seven hundred years of Dominican scholarship, and nobody ever heard of us until we put five kids on the floor of Madison Square Garden."

One

Early New England Dominance: 1920–1944

On September 17, 1919, a new school opened its doors and welcomed an incoming class of 71 students and nine faculty members. On the very first day of classes, an informal game of basketball was organized. Today, many consider that event to have been prophetic.

Providence College attempted to field basketball teams in 1920 and 1921, but these teams were poorly organized; they had no coach, no practice facilities, and no home court. Both years, ambitious schedules were abandoned after only a few games, and these squads are not recognized as varsity teams.

After a three-year period that the school experienced a measure of success in baseball and football, it decided to attempt basketball again. The college's first varsity team—mostly made up of athletes from other sports—began competition in the 1926–1927 season. They were led by the school's football coach, Archie Golembeski.

When Golembeski resigned after only one season, the college hired Al McClellan, a highly successful high school coach. McClellan was a six-foot-six-inch giant who commuted daily from his home in Salem, Massachusetts. As a basketball coach, McClellan had few peers. By the program's third year of varsity competition, the Dominicans were the top team in New England and one of the best in the East.

Almost immediately, McClellan established the team and grabbed national attention with unexpected wins over recognized powers like St. John's University, Dartmouth College, and Villanova University. For nine years (from the 1928–1929 season through the 1936–1937 season), McClellan's team dominated the region and captured four New England championships (1929, 1930, 1932, and 1935) while finishing second in the region four other times (1931, 1933, 1934, and 1936). McClellan understood the necessity of competing outside of New England. In the 1920s and 1930s, he was the only coach in the region to challenge the top teams in the East, further enhancing his team's reputation.

By 1938, the school had decided to emphasize football and de-emphasize basketball. Rather than take a pay cut, McClellan resigned. In his place, the Friars hired Ed Crotty, a recent Notre Dame graduate. After two rebuilding years, Crotty began to revive the program. When football was dropped as a failed experiment in 1941, the basketball team reaped the benefits. By the 1942–1943 season, Providence College had its best material since the dominant McClellan teams, and the Friars were eyeing a possible invitation to the NIT.

World War II intervened and, as the season wore on, the Friars' star players began dropping off the team as they were called into the service. At the end of the season, with few students remaining on campus, the decision was made to suspend the college's sports program for the 1943–1944 academic year.

The decision was made to field a varsity basketball team, and the school began the process by establishing a freshman team in 1925. The freshman squad played a demanding 33-game schedule in the 1925–1926 season. They compiled a 19-10 record (the results of four games are lost to time). Shown, from left to right, are the following: (front row) Russell Wise, James McNeice, Ray O'Leary (captain), Ray Murphy, and Clement Spring; (back row) Frank Flynn, Gerard Dillon, Alfred Conti, and Frank Silva (coach). Only Spring and Dillon ever played varsity basketball for the Friars.

The 1926–1927 team was the first varsity squad. The team defeated Bridgewater State 31-19 on December 4, in the first-ever game. They then lost six in a row and went on to win seven of the final nine games, including a 36-33 upset at St. John's University. They finished off the season with eight wins and eight losses. Pictured, from left to right, are the following: (front row) Stan Szydla, Hector Allen (captain), and Charles Murphy; (back row) Thomas Bride (manager), Peter Rzeznikiewicz, John Murphy, Larry Wheeler, and Joseph Nole (assistant manager).

In 1925, Archie Golembeski was hired as the school's football coach. In a move not uncommon in those days, he was asked to coach the fledgling basketball team in its 1926–1927 season. A Holy Cross graduate, Golembeski guided the young Friars to a .500 record in his one year as coach and then stepped down in October 1927 to concentrate on football. He remained as the school's football coach until 1933.

Hector Allen (Class of 1928) was the first basketball star at the college and a great all-around competitor. A three-sport athlete, Allen captained the first varsity basketball team and was the squad's leading scorer in 1927, with an average of 7.3 points per game.

Al "the General" McClellan was a highly successful high school coach from Salem, Massachusetts, when he assumed control of the college's program in 1927. Eleven years later, the Friars had won almost 70 percent of their games and four New England championships. During the 1920s and 1930s, the General was the only New England coach willing to take his team outside of the region to face eastern powers in New York, New Jersey, and Philadelphia.

During the 1927–1928 season, the Friars had three players on the squad from Ware, Massachusetts. Adelard Fleurent (left), Stan Szydla (center), and Peter Rzeznikiewicz (right) all hailed from that town. Szydla was a four-year starter.

The 1928–1929 team was the school's first great squad. Early in the season, the team swept regional powers Dartmouth and Yale on the road and then gained national notoriety by surprising the St. John's University "Wonder Five" in Brooklyn. The team finished 17-3 and ranked third in the east and first in New England, despite playing only two home games. Pictured, from left to right, are Larry Wheeler, William McCue, Eddie Wineapple, Willard Cooley, Chick Gainor, George Cody, Ed Derivan, John Krieger, Stan Szydla, Jim Welch, John McCormac, and Al McClellan (coach).

During the early years, a persistent problem for the program was the lack of a home court. In this 1929 photograph, James Welch (left), Willard Cooley (center), and William "Chick" Gainor (right) practice outside the gym at nearby LaSalle Academy High School, which the college used on occasion for home games. Gainor achieved more fame as an amateur boxer than he did as a basketball player.

John Krieger arrived at Providence College from Paterson, New Jersey, in 1927. By the time he left in 1931, he owned the school's career-scoring mark with 742 points in 73 games. Krieger was the highest-scoring player in New England as a freshman and was runner-up as a sophomore and junior. A sharpshooting forward, John was a Second Team All-America pick in 1930 and 1931.

Eddie Wineapple played for McClellan at Salem High, matriculated at Syracuse for his freshman year, and then transferred to Providence College. The unquestioned star of the great 1928–1929 team, Wineapple was a First Team All-America player and an All-East and New England Player of the Year selection. The second-highest scorer in the east, Wineapple's 13.9 point average would stand as a college record for 13 years. After only one year, Wineapple left to play professionally for the Syracuse Nationals. He also pitched briefly for the Washington Senators.

The 1928–1929 team was crowned New England champions after the season. It featured one of the college's all-time great starting fives: Eddie Wineapple, John Krieger, William McCue, Larry Wheeler, and Stan Szydla. Pictured, from left to right, are the following: (first row) James Welch, Szydla, Wheeler, Krieger, and Michael Foster; (second row) Al McClellan (coach), Wineapple, McCue, and Mark McGovern; (third row) Willard Cooley and George Cody; (fourth row) George Forrest and Ed Derivan; (fifth row) Louis Imbriano (manager) and John Farrell (graduate manager).

William McCue played high school basketball with John Krieger and matriculated to Providence College with his lifelong friend. McCue was the playmaker on the great 1929 squad and, although he was not known for his scoring, scored enough to keep defenses honest. McCue scored 392 points in 73 games and was named an Honorable Mention All-America player in his senior year (1930–1931).

Allan "Dick" Bracken was, without question, the Friars' most dominant player of the 1930s. The flashy Bracken made an immediate impact by leading the team in scoring as a freshman in 1930–1931 and continued as leading scorer for the next three years. A Second Team All-American in both 1932 and 1933, Bracken played both guard and forward. In 1934, he graduated as the school's all-time leading scorer with 773 points—a mark that would stand for 17 years.

The 1931–1932 Friars captured their third New England championship after earning a 19-5 record that year. The 19 wins would stand as a school record for 27 years. The team also began playing home games against major opponents at the old Rhode Island Auditorium during this season. In this arena, they played against St. John's University and CCNY (City College of New York). Pictured, from left to right, are the following: (first row) John Glennon (manager), Ed Koslowski, Chick Gainor, Allan Bracken, and Al McClellan (coach); (second row) Fran Dromgoole, Ollie Roberge, Sam Shapiro, and George Cody; (third row) Frank Reavey and William Hyte; (fourth row) Birdie Tebbetts and Oscar Perrin; (fifth row) James Welch, Tom O'Brien (assistant manager), and John McCormick.

George "Birdie" Tebbetts was a little-used substitute on the 1931–1932 varsity basketball squad, scoring only six points in just four games. He was far better known for his baseball exploits, which included 14 years in the major leagues as a catcher with Detroit, Boston, and Cleveland, and 11 more years as a big-league manager.

In the 1932–1933 season, the Friars finished 13-3 and were led by this starting five. They are, from left to right, Ed Reilly, Sam Shapiro, Allan Bracken, Ed Koslowski, and Bill Kutniewski. They are gathered for a practice at their home court at Harkins Hall. The small gym doubled as an auditorium (note the stage behind the basket). Allen Bracken scored an average of 13 points a game, and Koslowski was impressive at center.

Bill Kutniewski was another of the school's great three-sport athletes. A senior captain in the 1934–1935 season, Kutniewski was the team's leading scorer at eight points a game and was an All-New England pick. The Friars posted a 42-13 record during Kutniewski's three varsity seasons.

Harkins Hall provided a huge home-court advantage for the Friars with its low ceilings and small-court dimensions. Students often crowded into doorways to watch practice, and priests and other fans observed from balconies. The Friars had a record of 60-8 when playing in Harkins Hall, from 1931–1946. Larger schools eventually refused to play there. In this 1934–1935 photograph, Al Hagstrom tries to pass to Joe Carew while Bill Kutniewski defends. In the background are Jim Bostick (5) and John Smith.

The 1934–1935 team finished 17-5 and won the fourth and final New England championship of the McClellan era. The Friars also began their home-and-home series with the University of Rhode Island this season and swept both games. Pictured, from left to right, are Al Hagstrom, John Smith, Bill Kutniewski, Joe Carew, Jim Bostick, and Al McClellan.

Basketball became an Olympic sport in 1936, and regional playoffs were held to determine a U.S. champion. The 1935–1936 team was 14-7 and was one of two New England teams (Springfield was the other) selected to play in a postseason Olympic playoff. The Friars lost to Springfield College 33-24 on March 12, 1936, in Cambridge, Massachusetts. Pictured, from left to right, are the following: (first row) Ed Bobinski, John Smith, and Leo Davin; (second row) Charles Gallagher and Joe Carew; (third row) Al McClellan (coach), Ray Belliveau, Charles Kelley, Carl Angelica, Al Hagstrom, and Ed Gill (manager); (fourth row) Bill Moge, Fred Collins, and Leo Ploski.

Until 1938, the rules stipulated that there would be a jump ball after every made basket. Teams with dominant centers usually won because they were able to control the ball. During McClellan's tenure, the Friars were fortunate to have, in succession, Larry Wheeler, Ed Koslowski, and Ed Bobinski playing center. Bobinski graduated in 1938 with 454 points in 50 games. He was a force inside.

Al "Gus" Hagstrom was a three-year starter for the Friars and scored 400 points in 63 games. After the class of Hagstrom, Leo Davin, and Joe Carew graduated in 1937, the Friars' fortunes sagged.

Mal Brown matriculated to Providence College in the early 1920s and assumed his role as the school's first athletic trainer a few years later. Brown was one of the most beloved figures on campus throughout the 1930s. In 1939, he died tragically in a typhoid outbreak. Today, the annual preseason scrimmage is named after him, as is the Mal Brown Award, given to the senior best personifying sportsmanship, courage, and honor.

Football and basketball player Ed Crotty graduated from Notre Dame in 1937. A year later, he was tabbed to be Al McClellan's successor as coach of the Friars. Crotty walked into a situation where basketball had been de-emphasized. However, he quickly began to rebuild the program. Just when he had the team challenging for top honors in the region, World War II began and the program was shut down. Crotty was forced to rebuild from scratch again. In 1946, he left after seven seasons to become the director of athletics for the town of Danbury, Connecticut.

By the 1941–1942 season, the program was on the rise again under coach Ed Crotty. On January 16, 1942, they collided with Rhode Island State (the top team in New England), coached by Frank Keaney. More than 5,800 fans (a record-breaking attendance for a New England college basketball game) saw the Friars upset the Rams 60-54 behind Ted McConnon's 18 points and Horace Marone's 14 points. The Friars finished the year 13-7.

Edward (Ted) McConnon played at St. Raphael's in Pawtucket and built his reputation as one of the outstanding shooters in college basketball in the early 1940s. In the 1941–1942 season, McConnon became the first Friar to record 300 points in a season and the first to average over 15 points a game for a season. He closed his two-year career in 1943 with a 15.3-points-per-game career scoring average. McConnon later became a highly successful coach at St. Anselm College.

The 1942–1943 Friars won their first eight games and were top-ranked in New England when they began to lose their stars to World War II. The team limped to the finish line with a 15-5 record, but it was the second highest scoring team in the nation. Seen here, from left to right, are the following: (front row) Ed Cariglia (manager), Henri Ethier, Ted McConnon, Bob Reilly, Chet Zabek, Larry Drew, and Joe Bagaglia; (back row) Ed Crotty (coach), Wilf Michaud, Al Palmieri, Ferdinand Sowa, Ben Pagliaroli, Bill Martin, and Dave Carberry.

Two

SMALL-COLLEGE STATUS: 1944–1955

By the fall of 1944, the tide had begun to turn in the war and many schools decided to restart their sports programs. At Providence College, that meant basketball would resume. With most of their stars still in the service, the Friars fielded an all-freshmen team and played a schedule made up mostly of service teams.

After the war, the landscape of college basketball changed dramatically. With the advent of the National Collegiate Athletic Association (NCAA) in the late 1940s, a distinction was made between a large-school division and a small-school division, a distinction that would soon become better known as Division I and Division II, respectively. With its small student population, the college fell into the small-school category. Gone from the team's schedule were the eastern powers (such as St. John's, Villanova, and Seton Hall) that they had played prior to the war. In their place were smaller schools like St. Anselm, Colby, and Bates.

Through the rest of the 1940s and into the early 1950s, the only large schools that the college played were regional rivals—the University of Rhode Island, Brown University, Holy Cross, and Boston College. The Friars usually endured lopsided defeats. Unable to attract talent because of their small-school status, the Friars bottomed out at 7-19 in 1949.

When Holy Cross won the national championship in 1947, Providence's new president, Fr. Robert Slavin, realized what a strong basketball squad could mean to a small Catholic school. At a conference in Philadelphia, he saw Catholic schools like Villanova and St. Joseph's packing fans into the Palestra. He knew the Friars would need a new home and a new coach.

A move was made to construct a basketball gymnasium for the Friars. For years, they had played in Harkins Hall. Throughout the 1940s, the Friars were nomads, playing in various city high school basketball courts. By 1952, ground was broken for a new state-of-the-art gymnasium, Alumni Hall, which would open in time for the 1955–1956 season.

In 1949, Slavin hired Vin Cuddy to begin the resurrection of the basketball program. Cuddy turned things around in his first year with a 14-9 record and quickly had the Friars playing in several small-school postseason tournaments. By 1954–1955, Cuddy's Friars had slipped to a 9-12 record, and he offered his resignation. While nobody knew it at the time, the Friars were ready to step onto college basketball's big stage as Alumni Hall was set to open.

When the Friars resumed playing basketball in January 1945, they returned with a team made up of all freshmen. It was the smallest squad in the country. Playing mostly service teams, the Friars compiled a 5-7 record. Seen here, from left to right, are the following: (front row) Bob Corry, Ted Horan, Leo Labossiere, John Arzoomanian, Dick Whelan, and John Boyle; (back row) Ed Crotty (coach), John Carr, Roger Dwyer, Joe Parente, Jean Mandeville, B. Grossi, Ted Daley, Hubert Dolan, and P. Connolly (manager).

By the 1946–1947 season, Harkins Hall was deemed inadequate for anything but practice, and the team began playing in the gymnasium at Central High School. The Friars were also reduced to playing a small-school schedule for the most part. Here, Paul McCormack drives against a St. Anselm College player in the season opener, a 67-59 win at Central High School's gymnasium.

Larry Drew was a prewar star at Providence College, earning Honorable Mention All-America honors for the 1941–1942 season. He then served in World War II. Drew completed his eligibility in 1946 and was named Friar coach to succeed Ed Crotty. Drew coached three unsuccessful seasons at the college and then stepped down after the program had bottomed out with a 7-19 record for the 1948–1949 season.

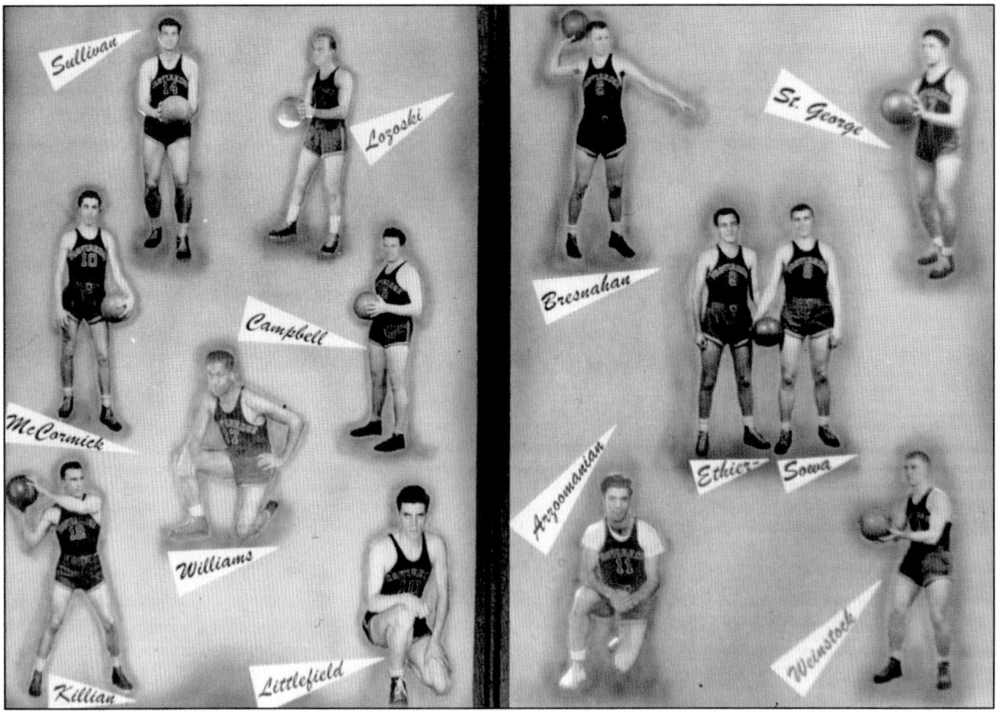

This unusual 1946–1947 team photograph shows the Friars with some talent, as several veterans returned from the service. John Sullivan was a talented center. John Arzoomanian averaged 19.7 points per game in 1945 and had scored a school record of 35 points that year against Hedron. Henri Ethier set a Boston Garden record with 34 points against St. Michael's in the 1945–1946 season, and Ferd Sowa was a talented scorer. Still, the team finished 8-11 that year.

Fr. Robert Slavin, O.P., was the president of the college from 1947 to 1961, and his vision was for the school to be nationally recognized in basketball. Slavin had just seen Holy Cross win a national championship in basketball and, after attending a conference in Philadelphia and taking in a Big Five doubleheader, knew that small Catholic colleges could compete. He worked toward the building of Alumni Hall, hired Joe Mullaney, and died shortly after watching the Friars capture the NIT in 1961.

James "Vin" Cuddy was hired to replace Larry Drew in 1949, after the college inquired about the University of Connecticut's coach, Hugh Greer. Greer decided to stay in Connecticut but recommended Cuddy, a recent Husky graduate. Vin set the stage for future Friar success, leading the team to its first sustained postseason tournament experience, and won 75 games in six seasons. In his 32 years at Providence, he served many roles at the college, including sports information director, business manager, and associate athletic director.

Vin Cuddy's first team in 1949–1950 rebounded for a 14-9 record and received a bid to the National Catholic Intercollegiate Basketball Tournament, losing to the eventual champion, Siena College. Here, Frank Pelligrino (19) and Sam Nissel battle for a rebound in a 93-67 win against Bates College on December 17, 1949, at Mount Pleasant High School.

The 1950–1951 squad was co-captained by Melvin (Sam) Nissel, Francis Pelligrino, and Raymond Garcia. All three were productive scorers, with Pelligrino tallying 626 points and leading the team as a sophomore in 1949. Nissel scored 575 points in his career there, and Garcia scored 569 points. The team finished 14-10 and received a bid to the National Athletic Intercollegiate Basketball Tournament.

The 1950–1951 Friars were selected to play in the National Athletic Intercollegiate Basketball Tournament. They captured the New England regional championship by defeating St. Anselm College (54-50) and Tufts University (77-74). Here, Frank Pelligrino (22), Melvin (Sam) Nissel, and Ray Garcia accept the championship trophy after the Tufts win. This win led them to the nationals in Kansas City, where they lost to Morningside College of Sioux Falls, Iowa, 66-63 on March 13, 1951.

James Schlimm (Class of 1952) was a six-foot-three-inch center from Pennsylvania who anchored Vin Cuddy's first three teams. Known for his lefty hook shots, Schlimm became the school's first 1,000-point scorer, finishing with 1,078 points in 70 games. "Slim Jim" often battled against bigger centers but set school records with 376 points and a 15.7-points-per-game average as a junior in 1951.

Robert Moran was an immediate scoring star from Brooklyn who teamed with Schlimm in the 1951–1952 season to lead the Friars to a 14-9 record and another National Athletic Intercollegiate Basketball Tournament appearance. Moran smashed Schlimm's scoring marks, leading the team in Jim's final season, with an 18-points-per-game average. Moran's older brother, Jackie, played at Boston College, while his younger brother, Donnie, followed him to Providence.

Robert Moran anchored coach Vin Cuddy's Friars in the early 1950s and finished his career in 1954 as the school's leading all-time scorer. An excellent free-throw shooter, Moran averaged a school-record 20.8 points per game in the 1952–1953 season, and finished with 1,251 points. Alas, the Friars could only manage .500 records in Moran's junior and senior years.

On February 9, 1954, the Friars reached the 100-point mark for the first time in their basketball history. Robert Moran (19) scored 20 points, while Ralph Tedesco (22) had 31, and the Friars raced past the University of Rhode Island 101-81.

From 1949 to 1955, the team played its home games in the tiny gym at nearby Mount Pleasant High School. No more than 800 spectators could cram into the gym to watch the Friars. Here, six-foot-six-inch center John Ritch goes high for a rebound in a January 12, 1955 contest against Boston College while Lionel Jenkins, Mike Pascale (19), and Ken Kerr (20) look on. Friars fans had hope that things would improve, however, as a new on-campus gym was being built and was scheduled to open the following season.

Forward Mike Pascale was a three-year starter for the team and scored 1,035 points. An excellent foul shooter, Pascale is shown sinking a free throw in a 79-78 loss at Brown University on March 2, 1955. This was Vin Cuddy's last game as coach. The Friars finished the season 9-12.

Three

The Joe Mullaney Era: 1955–1969

When a president of another school asked Fr. Robert Morris, vice president at Providence College, how his school could emulate the Friar's success, Morris replied, "Very simple. Just go out and hire an obscure coach and have him turn out to be a basketball genius. And recruit some little-known players and have them end up as All-Americans."

The obscure coach for the Friars was Joe Mullaney, a Holy Cross graduate who had played on the Crusader's 1947 NCAA championship team and then played briefly for the Boston Celtics. At the time that he was tabbed to be Vin Cuddy's successor, Mullaney's only coaching experience was one year spent at tiny Norwich College in Vermont.

During Mullaney's first year at Providence College, the Friars sprung an attention-getting upset on the University of Notre Dame. By his third year, the team was on the verge of an NIT invitation. By his fourth year, the Friars were in the NIT and had captured the imagination of New York's basketball fans. By his fifth year, the Friars were in the NIT finals.

While Mullaney had his share of success recruiting well-known players like John Egan, Jim Hadnot, and John Thompson, the team's ultimate success hinged on little-known players like Lenny Wilkens, Ray Flynn, and Jimmy Walker, who blossomed after arriving on Smith Hill.

Mullaney, a master of late-game strategy, is credited with developing the match-up zone defense. The Friars became known as the Cardiac Athletic Club for their propensity to play heart-wrenching, down-to-the-wire games, the majority of which were won. Under Mullaney, the Friars also developed a David and Goliath reputation that exists to this day—the tiny school from Rhode Island that defeats the big basketball powers.

By 1960, the Friars were the dominant team in New England, a position that they would maintain for most of the next 20 years. Their annual NIT victories brought the school national attention, and Rhode Island went wild, turning out by the tens of thousands to welcome their team home after the 1961 and 1963 NIT championships. Under Mullaney, the team compiled a streak of nine straight 20-win seasons, an NCAA Elite Eight run in 1965, weekly rankings in the national polls, and an unmatched tradition of excellence. That it happened so fast was incredible. It seemed light years away from the early 1950s, when the team was operating at what today would be considered a Division II level.

When Mullaney left for the National Basketball Association (NBA) in 1969, the only question was if the success could continue.

Joe Mullaney was a young, unproven coach when he was hired as the Friars' sixth coach in 1955. By the time he left for the NBA in 1969, he had compiled a 271-94 record and led the Friars to two NIT championships and a NCAA Elite Eight appearance. Mullaney is credited with developing the match-up zone. He produced six All-Americas, had nine consecutive 20-win seasons, and put Providence basketball on the map, establishing the school as the power in New England and a perennial Top 20 team.

After three years of construction, Alumni Hall opened in time for the 1955–1956 season, and Providence had a true on-campus home court at last. The Friars inaugurated Alumni Hall with a game against crosstown rival Brown University on December 3, 1955. In front of a sold-out crowd, center John Ritch (shown shooting) led the Friars to a 71-55 victory. Also playing for Brown was future Providence College assistant athletic director Gerry Alaimo.

The Friars wanted a marquee game for their inaugural season in Alumni Hall, and so they scheduled the University of Notre Dame for a February 14, 1956 tilt. The Friars surprised the Fighting Irish by jumping to an early lead, but Notre Dame battled back, and the game was tied at 73 at the end of regulation time. With most of the Friars' regulars having fouled out, little-used substitute Gordie Holmes took an inbound pass from Frank Williams near half court (above) and launched a 45-footer that swished through at the buzzer (below). The Friars had an improbable 85-83 overtime win over Notre Dame, and Providence College basketball was back on the map.

Lenny Wilkens arrived virtually unknown after playing less than a season of high school basketball at Boys High in Brooklyn, New York. Recommended to Joe Mullaney by his parish priest, Father Mannion, Wilkens developed into one of the school's all-time greats. A First-Team All-America as a senior, Wilkens was a versatile scorer on offense and a smothering pickpocket on defense. He led the Friars to an 18-6 record in the 1957–1958 season. The previous season, Wilkens, along with Wally DiMasi, John Woods, and Richard Whelan, had led the freshman team to an undefeated season, signaling a bright future for the program.

John Egan was the best high school basketball player in New England at Weaver High in Hartford, Connecticut, and was Joe Mullaney's first big-name recruit. He had a spectacular career at Providence College, averaging 20.9 points per game as a sophomore in 1958–1959 and scoring 1,434 career points. Never quite the same after a knee injury following his sophomore season, Egan still earned Honorable Mention All-America notice in 1959 and 1961, and the guard led the team to the 1961 NIT championship.

On January 24, 1959, the Friars traveled to the Palestra, in Philadelphia, to play 19th-ranked Villanova University. Friars fans listened to the Friars for the first time on the radio, as Johnny Egan scored a Palestra and school record of 39 points in a stunning 90-83 four-overtime win over the Wildcats. The signature win propelled the Friars to its first-ever NIT invitation.

When the team faced pre-tournament favorite St. Louis University in the 1959 NIT quarterfinals, no one gave them a chance against the much taller Billikens, led by All-American Bob Ferry. The New York press dubbed the Friars "Mullaney's Midgets" because no starter was taller than six feet, five inches. The team quickly became the fan favorites. John Egan (11) is shown sinking the final basket of the game in Providence College's stunning 75-72 double-overtime win.

The Friars' locker room is jubilant after their upset win over St. Louis. School president Fr. Robert Slavin is shown congratulating coach Joe Mullaney. The Friars' run would end in the next game, which was a 76-55 loss to 17th-ranked St. John's. That year, the team finished 20-7, for the program's first 20-win season.

In the 1959–1960 season, a giant 6-foot-10-inch center began his varsity career after being a standout at McClymonds High in Oakland, California. Jim Hadnot gave the Friars their first true big man, and Hadnot is shown signing an autograph for a young fan before his second varsity game, a 84-53 win at Brown on December 9, 1959. Hadnot scored 1,467 points and grabbed 1,299 rebounds in a stellar career that saw him named Honorable Mention All-America twice.

The Friars hosted their own holiday tournament in 1958–1959 and 1959–1960, winning the championship both times. Here, Lenny Wilkens accepts the tournament's MVP award from athletic director Father Begley and head coach Joe Mullaney after the 1959–1960 final. Wilkens scored 25 points and grabbed 10 rebounds as the Friars swept past Georgetown University 83-56 to claim the tournament crown.

The Friars returned to the Palestra on January 23, 1960, to face 20th-ranked St. Joseph's. In another nail-biter, the team prevailed 64-63, as Lenny Wilkens stole the ball game. With St. Joseph's University up by three and just over a minute left, Wilkens stole the ball on three consecutive possessions (twice from All-American Bobby McNeil, once from Paul Westhead) and converted two baskets for the Friars' upset. The win pushed the team into the Top 20 for the first time ever.

Providence accepted their second straight NIT bid and would travel to Madison Square Garden to face Memphis State in the first round. Here, Providence College students urge their team on with a handmade sign. The Friars obliged, edging Memphis State 71-70 on March 15, 1960.

The team reached its first NIT championship final in 1960 and had the top-seeded and nationally fourth-ranked Bradley Braves on the run. With 10 minutes to play, the Friars held a 12-point lead but began forcing shots and were outscored 38-10 down the stretch. All-American Chet Walker skied for rebounds like this one, despite pressure from Dick Leonard (43) and Denny Guimares. When it ended, Providence (24-5) lost in an 88-72 defeat.

After the season, Lenny Wilkens became the first Friar selected to play in the prestigious East-West All-Star game at Madison Square Garden, featuring the top seniors in the country. Here, Wilkens, who would be named the game's co-MVP, has just stolen the ball with eight seconds left and his team down by one. Wilkens then sinks the winning shot for the East. Second from the left is Oscar Robertson.

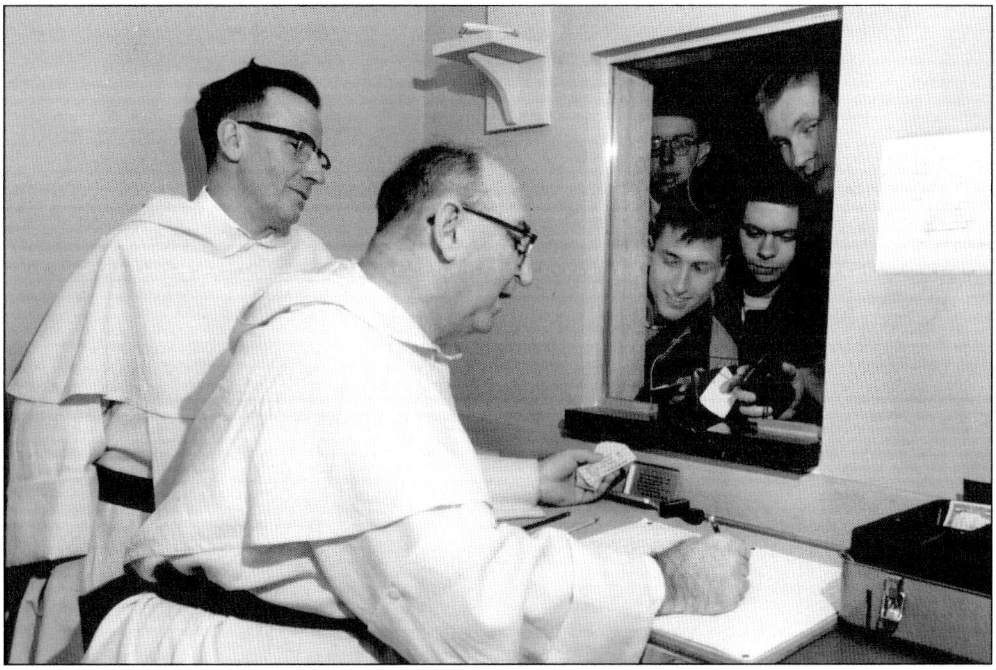

By the 1960–1961 season, tickets to a game had become a hot item. The athletic director, Fr. Aloysius Begley, took a personal interest in promoting the school's basketball team. Begley served as athletic director from 1941 to 1971. He was instrumental in the hiring of Joe Mullaney as coach and the building of Alumni Hall.

On February 2, 1961, the Friars hosted the Creighton Blue Jays and rolled to a whopping 115-70 win. Two Friars, John Egan (with the ball) and Jim Hadnot (54), each scored 31 points. The team's 115 points set a school record that would stand for 12 years.

Rhode Island was awash in Friar fever as the team prepared to travel to New York for its third NIT appearance. Billboards like this one were everywhere, wishing the Friars luck.

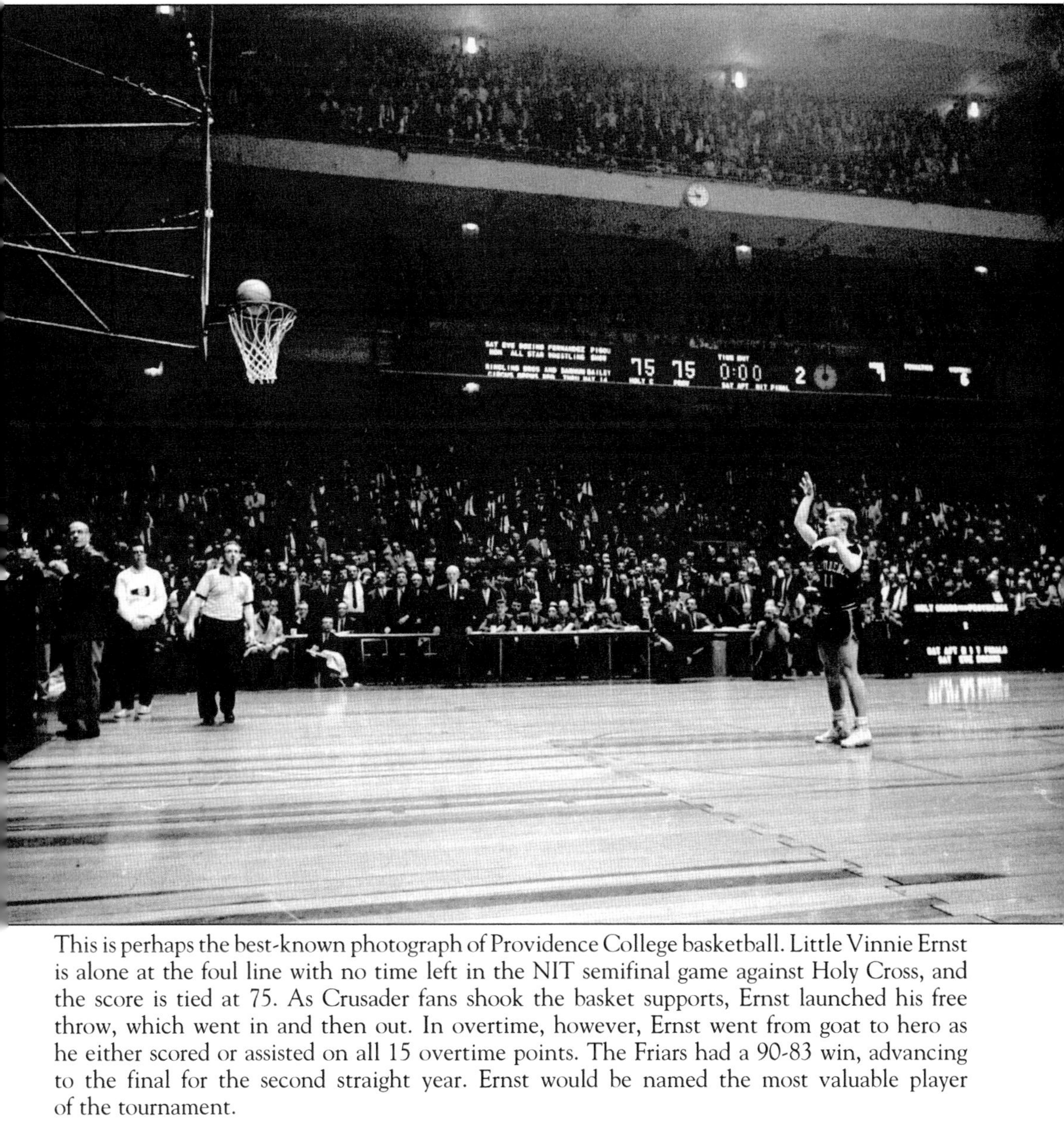

This is perhaps the best-known photograph of Providence College basketball. Little Vinnie Ernst is alone at the foul line with no time left in the NIT semifinal game against Holy Cross, and the score is tied at 75. As Crusader fans shook the basket supports, Ernst launched his free throw, which went in and then out. In overtime, however, Ernst went from goat to hero as he either scored or assisted on all 15 overtime points. The Friars had a 90-83 win, advancing to the final for the second straight year. Ernst would be named the most valuable player of the tournament.

In the NIT championship game, on March 25, 1961, the team found itself facing a familiar foe. St. Louis University, ranked 14th, was the opposition, and the Friars trailed by seven with 10 minutes to go. Sophomore power forward George Zalucki (shown here battling for a rebound) played the best game of his career with 17 points and 10 rebounds, and the Friars rallied for a 62-59 win. They had finally conquered the NIT and were at the top of the college basketball world.

Jim Hadnot stands out in the crowd of the Friars' victory celebration after returning home from the 1961 NIT. Rhode Island went crazy for the victorious Friars and turned out by the thousands for a tribute to the team in front of city hall. Thousands more had lined the bus route from the Connecticut border all the way to downtown Providence to welcome the Friars home.

The 1960–1961 team captured the school's first NIT championship and raced to a 24-5 record. Pictured, from left to right, are the following: (front row) Jim Swartz (assistant coach), Vin Ernst, Tom Folliard, Tim Moynihan, John Egan, Dennis Guimares, Ray Flynn, and Joe Mullaney (coach); (back row) Tom Drennan (manager), Dick Leonard, Carl Spencer, Tom Nyire, Jim Hadnot, George Zalucki, Rich Holzheimer, and Peter Louthis (trainer).

Preseason polls had the Friars picked fourth in the nation in 1961–1962. They had just won the NIT and were adding 6-foot-10-inch sensation John Thompson. However, twin towers Jim Hadnot (with ball against the University of San Francisco in a 72-63 early-season win) and Thompson never meshed to provide the team with a dominating inside presence. The Friars fell far below expectations with a 20-6 record and a first-round NIT exit.

Even the Friars practices were entertaining, as the team was loaded with talent. Jim Hadnot, Vin Ernst (point guard), and John Thompson put on a passing show during drills at Alumni Hall in the 1961–1962 season practices.

John Thompson arrived at the college after an All-America high school career in Washington, D.C., and played forward as a sophomore before moving to center for his final two seasons. Thompson, who later gained fame as Georgetown University's coach, scored 1,520 points and grabbed 1,061 rebounds, while gaining First Team All-America mention. More mobile than Hadnot, Thompson had a sensational senior season, averaging 26.2 points per game and scoring a school-record 43 points against Fairfield University.

John Thompson goes high to dunk during a December 14, 1962 visit from St. Louis University. The Friars downed the Billikens 64-57 at Alumni Hall. Bob Kovalski (54) and Vinnie Ernst (10) look on. Note the Dalmatian mascot on the left.

Ray Flynn (left) and Vin Ernst (right) teamed to give the Friars a formidable backcourt in the early 1960s and led the team to two NIT championships. Flynn was a superb deep shooter who scored 1,025 points and later became the mayor of Boston. Ernst was a tricky five-foot-seven-inch ball handler who quarterbacked the Friars and handed out 487 assists to go along with 911 career points.

On February 12, 1963, the Friars defeated the University of Rhode Island 93-75 for coach Joe Mullaney's 150th win. Here, longtime trainer Pete Louthis and assistant coach Dave Gavitt look over Mullaney's shoulder as Joe cuts the cake.

The Friars moved on to the NIT for the fifth-straight year. In the first round, the Friars faced the tough University of Miami team that had beaten them earlier in the season. They jumped out to a big lead, but Miami roared back, trailing by just four with one and a half minutes left. Miami's Rick Barry fouled Ray Flynn (shown here) and then slammed the ball to the floor and drew a technical. Flynn hit three free throws and iced the game 106-96 for the Friars. Flynn led the way with 38 points and was named the tournament's most valuable player.

Providence College captured its second NIT championship with an 81-66 win over Canisius College on March 23, 1963. The 24-4 Friars had lost to Canisius earlier in the season by an 80-75 count, and so they were able to avenge two of their four losses during the season in this tournament.

For the second time in three years, thousands of Friars fans lined Route 6 from the Connecticut border all the way into downtown Providence to welcome home the bus carrying the Friars.

In a ceremony at the Rhode Island State House, Gov. John Chafee presents coach Joe Mullaney with a special license plate commemorating the team's NIT triumph.

The 1962–1963 Friars won their final 15 games of the year and captured their second NIT championship. The streak began with a comeback win (84-72) at Madison Square Garden over the University of Dayton on January 31. Pictured, from left to right, are the following: (front row) Joe Mullaney (coach), Noel Kinski, Vin Ernst, Ray Flynn, Bob Simoni, Bill Stein, and Dave Gavitt (assistant coach); (middle row) Jeff Shea, Jim Cox, Don Dutton, Jim Stone, and Jim Ahern; (back row) Bob Kovalski, John Thompson, Tom Nyire, and Carl Spencer.

Joe Mullaney handed the ball to seniors John Thompson and Jimmy Stone and they co-captained the 1963–1964 Friars to a 20-6 record and the school's first NCAA berth, losing to seventh-ranked Villanova University. Thompson averaged 26.2 points per game, while Stone averaged 19.5 points per game. A six-foot-two-inch forward, Stone had a bad knee and played with a brace but scored 968 points in his career. Mullaney called him "the best one-legged player in America."

In the 1964–1965 season, Joe Mullaney had one of his most talented teams. Bill Blair, Jim Benedict, Jimmy Walker, and Dexter Westbrook helped lead the team to a 19-0 start, before losing to Villanova. The Friars reached number three in the polls during their streak. Walker and Westbrook, along with Mike Riordan, had arrived to the varsity from an undefeated freshman team (21-0) the year before.

Dexter Westbrook was a talented six-foot-eight-inch center who had played with Jimmy Walker at Laurinburg Academy in North Carolina prior to arriving at Providence College. Westbrook (shown here shooting in a 102-75 win over the University of Massachusetts on March 2, 1965) averaged 14.4 points per game and 12.2 rebounds per game in his one year with the team. After the season, Westbrook left for academic reasons.

James Benedict was another in a long line of excellent outside shooters during the Mullaney years. Benedict scored 1,086 points during his career and was always a threat to score.

The 1964–1965 team finished 24-2 and ranked fourth in the nation. The Friars reached the Eastern Regional finals of the NCAA Tournament but were blasted by Bill Bradley and Princeton University 109-69. Pictured, from left to right, are the following: (front row) Jim Benedict, Bill Lasher, Noel Kinski, James Ahearn, Dexter Westbrook, and Jim Schessler; (middle row) Jim Cox, Steve Sarantopoulos, Bill Blair, Jimmy Walker, and Don Dutton; (back row) Joe Mullaney (coach), Pete McLaughlin, Mike Riordan, Bill Barrett, David Turbridy, and Dave Gavitt (assistant coach).

Joe Mullaney had reason for optimism in the 1965–1966 season, even with the loss of Dexter Westbrook. Four starters were back from the previous season's Elite Eight squad, including Jimmy Walker (24), Mike Riordan (54), Bill Blair (14), and Jim Benedict (20). Bill Lasher (34) and Bob Kovalski (52), who was back from a year off due to academics, would handle the center spot. However, neither could replace Westbrook.

In the 1960s, the annual Holiday Festival, held at Madison Square Garden, was the most prestigious in-season tournament in the country. Winning it was almost as noteworthy as winning the NIT. The Friars captured the 1965–1966 Holiday Festival by downing New York University and the University of Illinois and then edging Boston College 91-86, behind Jimmy Walker's record-tying 50 points on December 30, 1965. For his efforts, Walker won MVP honors for the tournament.

Bill Blair is best remembered as Jimmy Walker's cousin. Indeed, Walker was discovered by the Friars when Blair's mother told Joe Mullaney, "If you think my son is good, you should see my nephew." But Blair was a high-flying, six-foot-three-inch forward whose talent stood on its own. Blair scored 801 points in his career and, in his senior year of 1965–1966, led the nation in free throw shooting at over 90 percent.

Mike Riordan (55) played his career in Jimmy Walker's shadow, but the six-foot-five-inch swingman provided a presence on the boards for the Friars and was a tenacious defender. Iron Mike scored 911 points and grabbed 663 rebounds in his career. Riordan is pictured battling against the Rhode Island Rams in Keaney Gym on January 11, 1966, in a 86-79 Friar win.

By 1965–1966, the Friars were Jimmy Walker's team and would go as far as he could take them. Walker averaged 24.5 points per game and garnered his first of two First Team All-America mentions as the team finished 22-5 and played in its third-straight NCAA Tournament. They lost to sixth-ranked St. Joseph's University in the first round. Here, Walker shoots against Niagara University in an 80-67 win on January 29, 1966. He scored 30 points in the game.

On December 30, 1966, Jimmy Walker won his second Holiday Festival MVP award as the Friars captured their second-straight tournament title. The team beat Duquesne University, Northwestern University, and then St. Joseph's University (82-76) for the championship. Walker scored 37, 38, and 25 points in the wins, respectively.

Jimmy Walker is congratulated by his teammates after sparking the Friars to a 82-76 win over St. Joseph's in the finals of the 1966–1967 Holiday Festival. Walker concluded his career with 2,045 points and led the nation in scoring at 30.4 points per game in the 1966–1967 season. He would then become the first and only player from a New England school to be picked number one in the NBA draft.

After watching his team struggle in the middle in 1965–1966, Joe Mullaney recruited center Tony Koski. At six feet, eight inches, Koski gave the Friars a presence at center and averaged 11.2 rebounds per game during his two seasons as a Friar. Here, he battles Brown for a rebound in a 77-68 win on March 4, 1967. The Friars would finish the season 21-7, with a spot in the NIT.

Al "Skippy" Hayes was a talented 5-foot-11-inch guard who attempted to pick up the slack after Jimmy Walker graduated. Hayes led the 1967–1968 team with a 15.6 points per game scoring average, but without Walker and Mike Riordan, the team slipped to 11-14. It was Joe Mullaney's worst record in his 14 years at the school.

The Friars rebounded in the 1968–1969 season with a 14-10 record behind players like captain Andy Clary (32) and Ray Johnson (52). Here, Clary takes the ball to the hoop against St. Bonaventure's Bob Lanier in the Friars' 70-59 upset over the 20th-ranked team on January 7, 1969.

Joe Mullaney's last hurrah in the 1968–1969 season included a hard-fought 98-81 loss to top-ranked University of California at Los Angeles (UCLA) in the Holiday Festival. Mullaney left Providence College to accept the head coach job with the NBA's Los Angeles Lakers.

Four

THE DAVE GAVITT ERA: 1969–1979

After the success of the Mullaney years, many were doubtful that the small school could continue at the same high level. There was always the perception that it all had somehow been just a fluke, lightning caught in a bottle. Furthermore, with Mullaney's departure, the magic ride was surely over.

Dave Gavitt had been an assistant coach working under Mullaney for four years, from 1962–1963 through 1965–1966. A Dartmouth graduate, he then returned to his alma mater to take over as head coach for Doggie Julian. After three years of reviving the Big Green's basketball program, Gavitt was a natural choice to succeed Mullaney, and he returned to Smith Hill. Few people realized that Gavitt was about to take the program to even greater heights.

By his second season, Gavitt began his own string of eight consecutive 20-win seasons, with as many postseason tournaments. The Friars reached the NCAA Final Four for the first time in 1973, reached the NCAA Sweet Sixteen in 1974, and played in their fourth NIT final in 1975. Once again, Providence was the dominant basketball program in New England.

Gavitt was also a visionary. Realizing that the program had outgrown Alumni Hall, he spearheaded a move to the new 12,000-seat Providence Civic Center, which opened in November 1972. There, the Friars could play a national schedule, and the sellout crowds would help to fund the school's entire athletic program. Not many schools were playing in large arenas at the time, and Providence College became the heart, soul, and undisputed capital of college basketball in New England.

The team began hosting its own holiday tournaments under Gavitt, and the Friars were the only eastern team to appear on national television during the 1970s. Like Mullaney, Gavitt was a great bench coach, and his style of play was dictated by his talent. Gavitt's teams pulled off 23 upsets of nationally ranked teams in his 10 years as Friar coach.

By 1978, the wear of being both the basketball coach and the school's athletic director (since 1971) was beginning to tell on Gavitt. Before the 1978–1979 season, shortly after being named the 1980 United States Olympic coach, Gavitt announced that the season ahead would be his last on the bench. He would split his attention between his duties as athletic director and commissioner of his greatest vision—the new Big East Conference.

Dave Gavitt was Joe Mullaney's assistant for four years, from 1962–1963 to 1965–1966, before leaving to become coach at Dartmouth. Three years later, when Mullaney stepped down, Gavitt was the natural choice to replace him. In 10 years with the Friars, Gavitt compiled a 209-84 record that included eight straight 20-win seasons and an NCAA Final Four team. Gavitt also lead the move to the Providence Civic Center and the formation of the Big East Conference. He was also the United States Olympic Coach in 1980.

Vic Collucci was an outstanding deep-shooting guard on Dave Gavitt's first teams. Collucci is best remembered for his 36-point performance against UCLA in the 1968–1969 Holiday Festival. He is also known for scoring 892 points in his career and averaging 13.9 points per game for the 1969–1970 Friars, who had a record of 14-11.

Ray Johnson was a six-foot-seven-inch center who was often forced to play against taller opponents, but he was the only height that Gavitt had on his first team. Johnson, shown here during an 81-78 loss to Dayton University on January 10, 1970, averaged 10.4 rebounds per game as a junior in 1969–1970 and pulled down 663 rebounds in his career. The Friars did pull off two big upsets during Gavitt's first year—against 16th-ranked St. John's and 19th-ranked Villanova.

In the 1970–1971 season, the Friars reclaimed the top spot in New England with a 73-72 win over the University of Massachusetts and the team's superstar, Julius Erving (32). The 5-foot-11-inch Donnie Lewis (20) shadowed the six-foot-seven-inch Erving throughout the game and battled him to a standoff. Meanwhile, Ernie DiGregorio (15) killed 45 seconds with a dribbling exhibition and then scored the last of his 33 points to give the Friars the win.

Ernie DiGregorio grew up idolizing Jimmy Walker and dreaming of playing for the Friars. After playing high school basketball at North Providence, DiGregorio attended St. Thomas More for a year and was recruited by Joe Mullaney. However, he never played for Mullaney. One of the most exciting Friars ever, DiGregorio was a magician with the ball and a First Team All-American as a senior in 1973, as he helped to usher in the Providence Civic Center era. He averaged 24.6 points per game as a senior and had 1,760 points and 662 assists in his career, still a school record.

The 1970–1971 Friars finished with a 20-8 record and grabbed an NIT bid. They polished off the University of Louisville 64-58 in the first round, before falling to top-seeded University of North Carolina, 86-79. Here, senior Jim Larranaga looks for an opening against Louisville. Larranaga scored 1,258 career points and played point guard, shooting guard, and small forward during his three-year career as a starter.

In the 1971–1972 season, Friar fans were thrilled by the arrival of six-foot-nine-inch center Marvin Barnes. A Providence native who had played at Central High School, Barnes gave Dave Gavitt his first legitimate big man. Marvin served notice of what was to come when he registered a triple-double in his second varsity game. He scored 13 points and recorded school records in rebounds (34) and blocked shots (12) in a 76-58 win over Buffalo State on December 8, 1971.

The Friars rolled through opponents in the 1971–1972 season and became firmly reestablished as the premier program in New England. Ernie DiGregorio took charge of the offense and averaged 17.7 points per game as a junior, along with delivering his usual assortment of electrifying passes for 214 assists. Teams such as St. Francis of New York (shown here during an 81-71 loss to the Friars on December 22, 1971) stood no chance against Providence College's team. The Friars finished with a record of 21-6 and lost to the University of Pennsylvania in the first round of the NCAA Tournament.

In their final game in Alumni Hall, the Friars played against St. John's on March 1, 1972, and came away victors in a 73-65 win. By the early 1970s, the 3,200-seat Alumni Hall was too small for the team. They moved to the new Providence Civic Center in their 1972–1973 season. The team compiled an impressive 178-29 record in Alumni Hall over 17 seasons. Here, senior defensive guard Don Lewis brings the ball up against St. John's University.

Providence kicked off a new era in Friar basketball when the team moved into the spacious 12,000-seat Providence Civic Center for the start of the 1972–1973 season. Junior forward Alan Baker is shown here scoring the final basket in the team's 93-57 dismantling of Fairfield University on December 11, 1972. It was the first game ever played in the Providence Civic Center. With stars like Ernie DiGregorio and Marvin Barnes, the team was a consensus preseason Top Ten pick.

On January 10, 1973, the Friars hosted Western Kentucky and beat the Hilltoppers 118-88, setting a new school record for points in a game. That record would stand until 1999–2000, when they scored 120 points against American-Puerto Rico. Senior Nehru King (30), a six-foot-six-inch forward, adds to the total with a free throw.

Providence traveled to Pauley Pavilion in Los Angeles on January 20, 1973, for a showdown with number-one-ranked UCLA, the defending national champions. The Bruins had won 58 straight, just two short of the record. John Wooden's team featured 6-foot-11-inch center Bill Walton, shown here guarding Ernie DiGregorio.

With both Marvin Barnes and Kevin Stacom (25) suffering from the flu, the Friars were crushed by UCLA, 101-77. Here, senior Fran Costello (31) battles Walton for a rebound. Costello was a sharpshooting, six-foot-eight-inch forward who played tough defense, passed well, and helped out on the boards. This loss would be the Friar's last of the season, before reaching the Final Four.

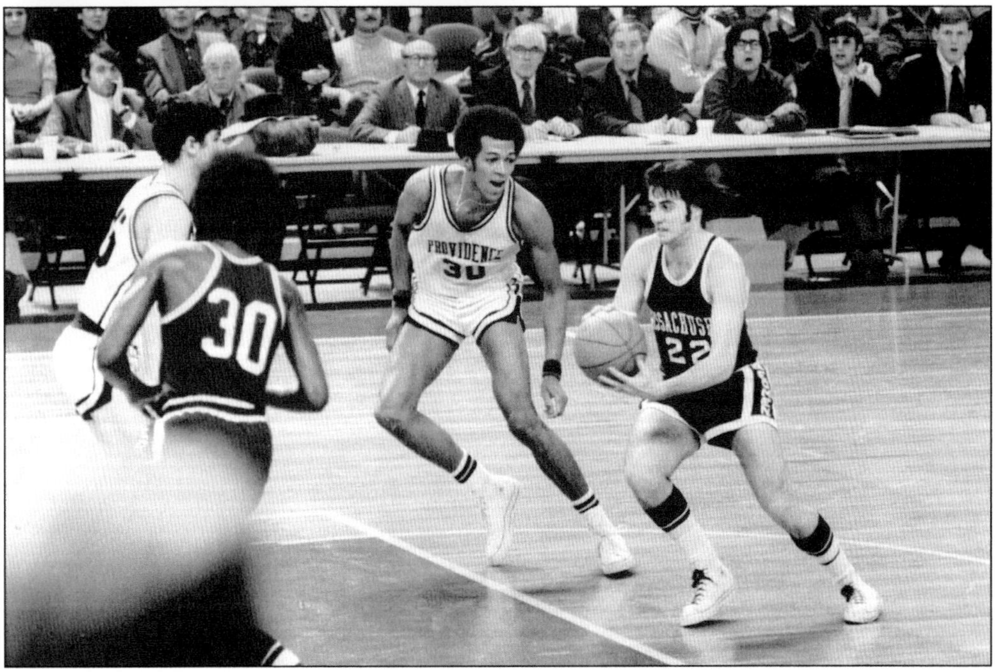

Before Rick Pitino became a highly successful college and professional coach, he was a point guard for the University of Massachusetts basketball team. Pitino (with the ball) faced off against Nehru King (30) and the Friars on January 24, 1973. The Massachusetts team lost to the Friars 91-78.

Thirteenth-ranked Jacksonville University rolled into the sold-out Providence Civic Center on January 27, 1973, and lost to the Friars in a thrilling 87-84 game. After the win, Ernie DiGregorio promised that the Friars would not lose again during the regular season, and he was right.

Kevin Stacom takes his turn cutting down the nets after the team's 103-89 win over the Maryland Terrapins in the Eastern Regional finals, in Charlotte, North Carolina. Stacom, a transfer from Holy Cross, teamed with Ernie DiGregorio to form one of the best backcourts in Friar history. Stacom averaged 17.8 points per game during his junior year. Stacom scored 24 points against the University of Maryland and keyed the Friars' second-half surge.

Ernie DiGregorio and Marvin Barnes share a drink after the Friars' thrilling upset win over Maryland in the 1973 Eastern Regional finals. DiGregorio scored 30 points before fouling out. Barnes and Kevin Stacom held the fourth-ranked Terrapins at bay as their team defeated Lefty Driesell's "UCLA of the East" and advanced to their first Final Four appearance.

The first eight minutes were a coach's dream. In fact, legendary CCNY coach Nat Holman called it "the best eight minutes of team basketball" he had ever seen. DiGregorio hit Kevin Stacom with a full-court, behind-the-back pass for a lay-up, and the Friars were running away from Memphis State 39-28. When Marvin Barnes injured his knee while coming down with a rebound, the Friars' run was over. Despite DiGregorio's 32 points, the Friars could not hold off the Tigers without Barnes inside. They lost 98-85, spoiling a rematch with UCLA in the championship game.

The 1972–1973 Friars are generally considered to be the best team the college has ever had. The Friars finished 27-4, ranked fourth nationally, and became the first team from New England to reach the Final Four since Holy Cross in 1947. Pictured, from left to right, are Dave Modest, Ron Norwood, Mark McAndrew, Nehru King, Charlie Crawford, Marvin Barnes, Fran Costello, Al Baker, Rich Dunphy, Kevin Stacom, Ernie DiGregorio, and Gary Bello.

Marvin Barnes was the most talented big man ever to wear the black and white. A dominating inside force, Barnes grabbed 20 or more rebounds in 29 different games throughout his career. After having the second-best average as a junior, he led the nation with an average of 18.7 rebounds per game as a senior. A First Team All-American in 1974, Barnes still holds the school's game, season, and career records for rebounds and blocked shots. He scored 1,839 points, grabbed 1,592 rebounds, and had 363 blocks.

Austin Peay State University invaded the Providence Civic Center on December 15, 1973. The university's star was Fly Williams, the nation's leading scorer. Although Williams lit up the Friars for 40 points, the game belonged to Marvin Barnes. Barnes earned a school record by scoring 52 points (he made 23 out of his 33 shots) and had 19 rebounds. However, the game was not decided until guard Rick Santos tipped in a shot at the buzzer to seal a 94-92 Friar win.

Bob Cooper burst onto the scene in the 1973–1974 season as a 22-year-old freshman from Chicago. The six-foot-seven-inch player provided help on the boards for Barnes and blocked 101 shots, which was the second-best record on the team. For his career, Cooper scored 1,424 points, pulled down 768 rebounds, and blocked 284 shots while splitting his time between forward and center. He will always be remembered for his 10 blocks against the University of Michigan as a senior.

Despite dominating New England college basketball in the early 1970s, the team did have a few challengers. On January 23, 1974, the Friars took on the second-ranked team in the region, Boston College. The game was a seesaw contest until, with seconds left, Kevin Stacom buried a jumper to lift the Friars to a 79-77 victory. After his game-winning shot, Stacom received a celebratory hug from freshman Joe Hassett (10).

Rick Santos, Bob Cooper, and Kevin Stacom share a laugh during a lighter moment in a season filled with overwhelming success. Santos had played with Marvin Barnes at Central High School and then attended Rhode Island Junior College, becoming the school's all-time leading scorer before arriving at Providence College. Stacom, who had played off-guard the previous season, switched to point guard during the 1973–1974 season to help offset the loss of Ernie DiGregorio. Stacom scored 1,143 points in just two seasons with the Friars.

The team rolled to a 28-4 record and ranked sixth nationally in the 1973–1974 season. The Friars reached the Sweet Sixteen of the NCAA Tournament. There, they ran into top-ranked and eventual national champion North Carolina State. Despite 40 points by David Thompson and 24 rebounds by seven-foot-four-inch Tom Burleson, the Friars hung tough, and the game was close until the five-minute mark. Foul trouble caught up with the team, and North Carolina State pulled away for a 92-78 win. Bob Cooper (shown here scoring) had 17 points and 10 rebounds.

With the departure of Marvin Barnes and Kevin Stacom, junior Mark McAndrew (a six-foot-five-inch swingman from Westerly) was one of the few veterans on the 1974–1975 team. McAndrew, who scored 712 points and amassed 519 rebounds in his career, was a tough, hard-nosed leader who always guarded the opposing team's best scorer. Here, McAndrew drives against Syracuse University in a December 14, 1974 game. The Friars topped the Orangemen 80-57, although Syracuse went on to reach the Final Four at the end of the season.

The young Friars battled to a 20-11 record in the 1974–1975 season and were picked for the NIT. In the first round, they faced top-seed Clemson University, with their seven-foot center, Tree Rollins. The underdog Friars, led by Bob Cooper (32) and Bill Eason (12), upset the Tigers 91-86. Suddenly hot, the team reached the NIT championship game by sweeping past the University of Pittsburgh and St. John's University but came up short against Princeton in an 80-69 loss.

On November 10, 1975, the Friars played the Russian National Team in an exhibition game. It was the same Russian team that had upset the United States in the 1972 Olympics. The Soviets led for most of the game, until a late Providence rally tied the score with seconds left. After receiving a pass from freshman David Frye, Joe Hassett (10) buried an outside jumper for a 76-74 win.

Playing in the Providence Civic Center allowed Dave Gavitt to schedule attractive intersectional games against teams like the University of Louisville, University of Oregon, and DePaul University. They were games that never would have been possible in Alumni Hall. On January 10, 1976, 16th-ranked Louisville came to town and lost 63-60, thanks to heroics by six-foot-nine-inch forward Bruce "Soup" Campbell, who led the Friars with 19 points and 12 rebounds.

Providence College's dormant rivalry with Holy Cross heated up again in the mid-1970s, as the Crusaders returned to the forefront with players like Chris Potter, Michael Vicens, and Ron Perry. For three years, starting in the 1975–1976 season, the Friars and Holy Cross staged several wars. On February 7, 1976, the Friars defeated Holy Cross 103-85, as erratic but talented guard Steve Strother (shown here reaching for the ball) torched Holy Cross for 25 points. Bob Cousy said of Strother, "He's the only player I've seen who can keep both teams in the game."

Picked for the 1976 NIT, the Friars' Bob Cooper helped the team dominate their first-round opponent, North Carolina A & T 84-68. The Friars then upset Louisville 73-67 before falling to Kentucky on a last-second, court-length drive for the game winner by Jack "Goose" Givens. After losing to the University of Kentucky 79-78, the team finished the season with a 21-11 record.

Providence College teamed with Industrial National Bank to host a holiday tournament in 1976–1977, and the Friars were fortunate to attract the top-ranked and undefeated University of Michigan. The Wolverines had been the national runners-up the year before and were favored to win it all in 1976–1977. Despite a heavy snowstorm, the Providence Civic Center was packed as the teams battled for the tournament championship. In a seesaw contest, Bob Misevicius nailed a jumper to send the game into overtime, and then, with time running out in the second overtime, Misevicius took a pass from Soup Campbell and buried a 12 footer for the Friar's 82-81 double-overtime shocker.

In postgame ceremonies, Bob Cooper and Joe Hassett were named to the all-tournament team. Cooper blocked 10 shots, and Hassett scored 21 points against the Wolverine's tough defense. Dave Gavitt joins his seniors to accept the championship award from bank chairman John Cummings.

Joe Hassett played high school basketball at nearby LaSalle Academy. As a freshman, he earned the nickname "Sonar" after hitting 90 percent of his long-range shots and sparking the Friars to a 67-62 win over St. Joseph's University at the Palestra. Generally considered to be the program's best outside shooter ever, Hassett scored 1,828 career points without the benefit of the three-point line (as the three-point line did not come into use until the 1986–1987 season). Joe led the team in scoring for three years, averaging 18.8 points per game as a senior in 1976–1977.

Bruce "Soup" Campbell was one of the top five high school players in the country after a sterling career at Wilbur Cross High in New Haven, Connecticut. The left-handed Campbell was a mobile, six-foot-nine-inch forward who was ahead of his time. A great ball handler and passer, Campbell scored 1,809 points and pulled down 949 rebounds in his career. He was named Honorable Mention All-America as a sophomore in 1976. Campbell was a good team player who often looked to create scoring opportunities for his teammates, at the expense of his own statistics.

The Providence College and University of Rhode Island rivalry was always passionate, but it turned ugly in 1976. The Friars had signed Sly Williams, a six-foot-seven-inch star from Lee High School in New Haven, Connecticut, to a non-binding letter, but Williams enrolled at the University of Rhode Island on the first day of school in a stunning development. Providence College officials were furious. The Rams' short-term gain may have cost them in the long-term, however. Two years later, the university was denied admittance into the Big East Conference. Here, Soup Campbell battles Williams for the ball in an 82-71 Friar win on January 18, 1977.

In the days before the shot clock, less talented teams would often hold the ball and refuse to shoot in an effort to keep the score down against a more talented team. Fairfield attempted that tactic against the Friars in the first round of the ECAC New England playoffs on March 3, 1977. The Friars prevailed, winning 44-31. In the process, however, they were thrown off their game and lost by a point to Holy Cross in the final. The Friars then lost to Kansas State 87-80 in the NCAA Tournament. They finished the season with a 24-5 record.

On December 9, 1977, during halftime of the team's 73-62 win over the University of Wisconsin, the school honored the longtime "Voice of the Friars," Chris Clark. Clark was responsible for getting Friar games on the radio. He personally paid the expense of having the 1958–1959 Providence-Villanova game from the Palestra in Philadelphia broadcast back to Rhode Island. After that thrilling game, sponsors lined up to be a part of broadcasts, and the rest of the games that season and thereafter were on the radio. Clark was also responsible for getting the games aired on local television. Clark called the Friar games on radio and television for 24 seasons.

Holy Cross was ranked 14th when they invaded the Providence Civic Center on January 18, 1978. For the most part, the Providence College and Holy Cross games were tight. In this contest, however, the Friars overwhelmed the Crusaders, winning 90-64. Senior center Bob "Big Beef" Misevicius, shown driving against Michael Vicens, shut Holy Cross down inside, and point guard Dwight Williams completely outplayed his rival Ronnie Perry, scoring 22 points.

By the 1977–1978 season, the University of Rhode Island was seeking the top spot in New England. On February 4, 1978, the college and the university clashed at the Providence Civic Center and the Friars came away the winners 79-59. Shown here going high for a dunk is freshman center Rich Hunger, who tormented the Rams off the bench with six points. The University of Rhode Island later captured the rubber match in the ECAC New England playoff finals with a 65-62 win.

Not even the Blizzard of 1978 could slow down the Friars. Gov. Joe Garrahy opened the airport to allow Dean Smith's North Carolina squad to fly in for a nationally televised game on February 12, 1978. The Friars stunned the seventh-ranked Tar Heels 61-59 before 7,000 dedicated fans. Here, junior forward Bill Eason (12) launches the last-second jumper that buried the Tarheels.

In 1974, Bill Eason, Soup Campbell, and Bob Misevicius made up the sixth-ranked recruiting class in the nation. By the time they graduated in 1978, they had won 89 games and lost 35. Eason was a six-foot-five-inch forward who scored 1,159 points and had 800 rebounds. Misevicius was the college's best-passing center ever. He scored 890 points, had 722 rebounds and an impressive 490 assists, and was great on defense. The 1977–1978 Friars finished with a 24-8 record. They lost to Michigan State, which starred freshman Ervin "Magic" Johnson, in the NCAA Tournament, 77-63. Although nobody knew it at the time, this season was the Friars' last hurrah for a while.

After 10 years as the college's coach, Dave Gavitt announced his retirement at the start of the 1978–1979 season. With all five starters gone from the previous year, the 1979 team would be Gavitt's weakest, which finished with a record of 10-16. The highlight of the season came in a rematch with the University of Rhode Island in Gavitt's last home game, on February 17, 1979. A month earlier, they had embarrassed the Friars 86-42. Now the Friars were looking for revenge. As the first half came to an end, six-foot-seven-inch sophomore forward Rudy Williams grabbed a rebound and launched an 89-foot shot that found the net and sparked the Friars to an 84-77 upset. At the time, Williams's shot was the longest in NCAA history.

Five

BIG EAST STRUGGLES: 1979–1985

Dave Gavitt understood that the future of college basketball was super-conferences and lucrative national television contracts. Throughout the 1970s, he had seen the landscape slowly change. When the NCAA Tournament began accepting multiple teams from leagues, thereby limiting the number of at-large berths, Gavitt knew that the future was bleak for the strong eastern independents, such as Providence College.

Gavitt began working behind the scenes to create what would be the first eastern super-conference, a league that would give the traditional eastern powers an opportunity to compete on a level playing field with the other respected leagues in other parts of the country, such as the Atlantic Coast Conference, the Big Ten, and the Southeastern Conference. A new eastern league would also aid in recruiting by helping to keep the best local high school players home.

One of the seven founding institutions, Providence College entered the new Big East Conference at precisely the wrong time. After 20 years of almost uninterrupted success, the Friars entered the league with their lowest level of talent in years and paid for it immediately.

To succeed himself as coach, Dave Gavitt tabbed Gary Walters, a young and energetic head coach at Dartmouth. Walters inherited a team that was short on talent and was forced to compete with programs on the rise, like Georgetown, Syracuse, and Villanova. The Friars failed to win a league game during their first year in the Big East Conference, and Walters resigned after only two years.

After eight successful years of coaching in the NBA and in the American Basketball Association (ABA), Joe Mullaney returned to the college ranks and was coaching at crosstown Brown University. Seeking to rebuild the Friars' suddenly tarnished reputation, Gavitt offered the job to his mentor, and Mullaney returned as the coach in 1981.

Realizing that he was at a severe talent disadvantage, Mullaney employed his trademark match-up zone and a slowdown offense in an attempt to stem the tide. The Friars pulled off a few upsets but fell short more often than not. During their first six years in the Big East Conference, the Friars' best conference mark was 5-11, their best finish was seventh, and their only winning record overall was 15-14 (in the 1983–1984 season).

When the team bottomed out at a school-worst (11 wins and 20 losses) in the 1984–1985 season, Mullaney decided to resign. The next hire would be crucial if the college was ever to break out of the second division of the league, and new athletic director Lou Lamoriello was determined to find the right person.

Dave Gavitt looked to his alma mater for the next Friar coach. Gary Walters was a young and energetic disciplinarian from Dartmouth, who walked into a program with little talent. In two seasons, Walters won only 21 games and just three in the Big East Conference. Best remembered for a run-in with star forward Rudy Williams over which socks Williams was wearing, Walters resigned after the 1980–1981 season.

Providence played its first-ever Big East Conference game at Georgetown University on December 18, 1979, losing 55-50. Here, Billy Fields congratulates Hoya coach and ex-Friar John Thompson after the game. Fields was one of the few bright spots for the team, scoring 1,116 career points, most of which were from long-range. The 1979–1980 Friars finished 11-16 and were winless in the new league, at 0-6.

Rudy Williams was a six-foot-seven-inch forward from Cambridge Rindge & Latin who scored 1,096 points and pulled down 577 rebounds in his Friar career. During Gavitt's last season, Williams was the team's leading scorer, averaging 17.8 points per game. However, his playing time decreased under Gary Walters, as he often clashed with the new coach. Here, he guards Duke University center Mike Gminski.

The InBank Classic scored another coup when they attracted top-ranked Duke to the 1979–1980 holiday tournament. The outmanned Friars hung tough with the Blue Devils, as Ricky Tucker (5) challenged Kenny Dennard's shot, while Bill Fields (35), Rudy Williams, and Jerry Scott (far right) look on. The team's upset bid fell just short, as the Friars lost 82-78 on December 22, 1979.

At the 1980–1981 InBank Classic, the Friars found themselves in the finals against the Michigan State Spartans. Jerry Scott, who seems to be trapped between Friars Marlon Burns and Sean Canty (22), torched the Spartans for 41 points, but the Friars came up short 77-76 on December 20, 1980. Scott, a high school teammate of Rudy Williams, closed his career with 1,045 points.

Joe Mullaney had returned to college coaching and was at Brown University when Dave Gavitt approached him about returning to Providence. Mullaney accepted and took over the Friar reins in March 1981. He found himself squaring off against one of his former players, John Thompson of Georgetown, on January 23, 1982, and the Friars upset 11th-ranked Hoyas 50-49.

Ron Jackson transferred in from Roxbury Junior College and made his presence felt immediately. The leading scorer for both of his varsity seasons, Jackson was a driving, spinning, outside-shooting guard who scored 971 points in two years. He teamed with Otis Thorpe (background) to give the Friars a semblance of an inside-outside attack.

Recruited by Gary Walters, 5-foot-10-inch point guard Ricky Tucker was a nonstop sparkplug who directed the team's offense for four years, piling up 520 assists, to go along with 819 points. What Tucker lacked in size he made up for in energy. Here, he drives against Chris Mullins in the Friars' 61-60 loss to St. John's University on December 4, 1982.

In the 1980–1981 season, because of commitments to their new league, the Friars began playing the University of Rhode Island once a year. The Governor's Cup was awarded to the game's winner. Here, the Friars celebrate an 81-69 win over the university on February 8, 1983, as the cup is given by Gov. Joe Garrahy to school president Thomas Peterson and guard Ricky Tucker. The Friars won four of the five Governor's Cup games.

On December 29, 1983, the team captured the Fleet Classic by downing the University of Pennsylvania and then beating Temple University 65-59 in the finals. Celebrating for the Friars are, from left to right, Dave Kipfer, Carl Hill, Jacek Duda, Billy Donovan, Dick Pennefather, Harold Starks, Ray Knight, Otis Thorpe, Alan Roth, and Donnie Brown. Although the team did not have much to celebrate in the early 1980s, they finished with a winning record of 15-14.

Otis Thorpe was one of the few bright spots for the Friars during the dark, early years of their membership in the Big East Conference. Thorpe was a 6-foot-10-inch center who scored 1,625 points and had 902 rebounds in his career. He was often forced to battle alone against players like Patrick Ewing, Ron Seikely, and Ed Pinckney. The Friars' only winning record from 1978–1979 to 1984–1985 occurred in Thorpe's senior year.

The 1984–1985 season started on a strong note as the Friars captured the Chaminade Invitational by downing the University of Virginia. Upon returning home, the team gave fans a preview of the dismal season ahead by dropping a 70-67 contest to Assumption College, a Division II team. Harold Starks, dribbling past Greyhound defenders, was a tough defensive-minded point guard who amassed 207 career steals to go along with his 706 points.

Freshman Matt Palazzi provided one of the few glimmers of hope on Mullaney's last team. Palazzi scored 819 points during a troubled Providence College career that ended in 1989. Mullaney, meanwhile, resigned near the end of a disastrous 11-20 campaign. After putting the program on the map during his first stint at the school, Mullaney's record during his second tenure was only 48-70, 14-48 in the league.

Six

RETURN TO PROMINENCE: 1985–2001

Rick Pitino arrived at Providence in March 1985 and immediately predicted that the Friars would soon be cutting down the nets. The little-known Pitino had coached at Boston University and had been an assistant with the New York Knicks. He was considered one of the young, rising stars in the coaching ranks.

Taking the same talent that had finished 11-20 in 1985, Pitino's first squad was invited to the NIT. His second team raced through the Big East Conference with a 10-6 record and then became a Cinderella team, pressing and three-point-shooting their way to their second Final Four appearance. After the season, with no athletic director in place, Pitino stunned the school by leaving to take the head coaching job for the Knicks. Still, Pitino had proven that the Friars could win in their conference, and he had provided the blueprint.

Pitino's decision unwittingly started a reputation that would last for a decade: Providence as a school that could not keep its coaches. After one turbulent season with Gordie Chiesa at the helm, Rick Barnes was hired in 1988. Barnes was another young, up-and-coming coach from George Mason University. Barnes was from North Carolina, and he never hid his intentions about returning to a southern school. He attempted to leave for the University of Virginia after two seasons. Persuaded to stay by Dave Gavitt, Barnes proceeded to lead the Friars to the 1994 Big East Conference Tournament championship. He then left for Clemson University after six years with the college.

The Friars' next choice for coach turned out to be Pete Gillen, a highly successful and established coach at Xavier University in Ohio. Gillen started his tenure with two trips to the NIT and then guided a talented team in 1996–1997 on a run to the NCAA Elite Eight. Gillen was unable to follow up on that success and, after a losing season in 1997–1998, he departed for Virginia. He had spent just four seasons coaching the Friars.

Providence College's basketball program was in desperate need of coaching stability when the school hired Tim Welsh in March 1998. The program had been through five coaches in 13 seasons, and fans openly wondered if the college was destined to be nothing more than a stepping-stone program, a developer of young coaches for bigger programs with more resources.

Welsh immediately had the Friars back in the NIT. After a tumultuous year (on and off the court) in 1999–2000, the Friars broke a school record of 11 Big East Conference wins and made the NCAA Tournament in the 2000–2001 season. After the season, Welsh signed a seven-year extension, and the school committed to much needed improvements in the facilities. After years of instability, the future looked bright indeed.

Rick Pitino arrived in Providence in March 1985 and promised an immediate turnaround. Pitino instituted "Midnight Madness" at the school in October 1985, making Providence one of the first schools in the country to kick off the season in this manner. At the first celebration, 100 fans showed up at midnight for a champagne toast. In later years, the event would grow far more popular and extravagant.

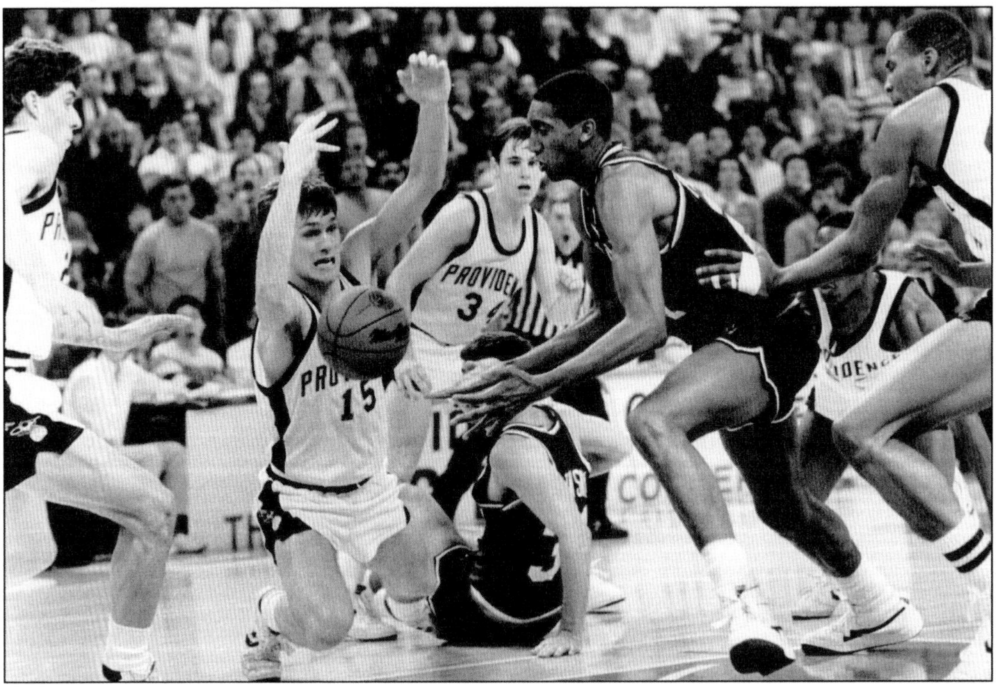

Rick Pitino's tough practices, insistence on conditioning, and nonstop press defense brought positive results quickly, but not without some struggles. Before tasting success, the Friars had a number of near misses. They lost 78-77 in double overtime to Villanova, on January 11, 1986. Dave Kipfer (15) and Billy Donovan (34) were two Friars who benefited greatly from Pitino's approach. Donovan emerged as a star in his junior year, averaging 15.1 points per game.

A 76-75 win over Boston College in mid-January gave the Friars their first taste of success, and the team never looked back. The Friars beat a good University of Pittsburgh team 76-67 on February 19, 1986. Shown at that game are backcourt partners Billy Donovan and Don Brown as they embrace in front of trainer "Fast" Eddie Jamiel (with ball).

By the end of the season, the team would finish 17-14 and a respectable 7-9 in the league, a far cry from the 11-20 record of the year before. The Friars also received an NIT bid, their first postseason appearance since 1978. They hosted three tournament games, beating Boston University and George Mason University before dropping a 64-63 contest to Louisiana Tech when Matt Palazzi's last second jumper would not drop.

Rick Pitino's stay at Providence was for only two years, but he is credited with turning the program around and leading the team back to postseason play. His frenetic full-court pressing defenses and reliance on the three-point shot, which was new in 1986–1987, took opponents by surprise and led the Friars to the Final Four. His Big East Conference record was 17-15 in two years, and he was 42-23 overall.

Delray Brooks transferred in from the University of Indiana with a reputation of having been one of the top high school players in the country. He became eligible in December 1986 and immediately teamed with Billy Donovan in the backcourt to give the Friars a potent outside attack. Brooks, shown scoring against Howard University in a 93-84 win on December 22, 1986, scored 781 points in his two years with the Friars.

Billy Donovan developed from a pudgy, slow point guard as a freshman to an All-American as a senior under Rick Pitino's watchful eye. The intense "Billy the Kid" drove the lane with abandon, bombed in 97 three-pointers as a senior, and was Pitino's coach on the floor. In his career, he scored 1,328 points and dished 546 assists. He averaged 20.6 points per game in the 1986–1987 season.

Few players in the team's history have played with the passion and intensity of six-foot-seven-inch forward Dave Kipfer (15). Another of the players who played listlessly prior to Pitino's arrival, Kipfer blossomed in his junior and senior seasons, epitomizing the heart and desire of the game. Originally from Canada, Kipfer scored 795 points and battled for boards for the Final Four Friars.

The Friars were searching for respect and, on January 28, 1987, while hosting eleventh-ranked Georgetown University, they found it. On a five-game winning streak, the Friars hung tough. When Ernie "Pop" Lewis nailed two three-pointers, the score was tied at 79 points. Here, Lewis launches the final shot of the game (another three-pointer) that would bury the Hoyas 82-79. When the team defeated 15th-ranked St. John's University 93-81 in overtime three nights later, they would move into the Top 20 for the first time since February 1978.

After the Friars' 97-80 win over Villanova on March 2, 1987, Rick Pitino is gathered with his seniors at half court. The players are, from left to right, Jacek Duda, Pop Lewis, Billy Donovan, and Dave Kipfer. The improvement in all four was dramatic. After the Big East Conference Tournament, the team was rewarded with an NCAA bid.

The Friars swept four NCAA games, beating the University of Alabama at Birmingham 90-68 on their opponent's home court. They edged Austin Peay State University in an overtime thriller 90-87 and then crushed ninth-ranked University of Alabama 103-82. The Friars surprised fourth-ranked Georgetown in the Southeast Regional final 88-73. The Friars were on their way to their second Final Four appearance, which was held in the Louisiana Superdome.

Before 65,444 fans, the team fell short in their bid to reach the NCAA championship game. Their perennial nemesis, Syracuse University, stopped them for the third time in the season. The Friars lost 77-63 in the semifinals, although freshman point guard Carlton Screen, with a team-leading 18 points, emerged as a future star on college basketball's biggest stage.

The 1986–1987 Friars finished 25-9 and 10-6 in the Big East Conference. They led the nation in three-point field goals, averaged 87 points per game, and shot 77 percent from the free-throw line. Shown, from left to right, are the following: (front row) Dave Kipfer, Jacek Duda, Billy Donovan, and Ernie Lewis; (back row) Carlton Screen, Bryan Benham, Delray Brooks, Abdul Shamsid-Deen, Marty Conlon, Steve Wright, Darryl Wright, James Best, and Ryan Ford.

When Rick Pitino surprised everyone by leaving for the New York Knicks, the Friars turned to top assistant Gordie Chiesa. Questions arose almost immediately after an early 99-98 loss to Holy Cross, and sophomore Marty Conlon left the team in early January. When the Friars slipped to an 11-17 record, Chiesa was let go after only one season, amid reports of further possible player defections.

The highlight of the disappointing 1987–1988 season was a January 16 visit from 13th-ranked University of Nevada at Las Vegas. The Friars hung tough for a half, but their opponents, led by Jerry Tarkanian and Stacy Augman, pulled away for a 92-72 win. Carlton Screen played well but spent most of the season in Chiesa's doghouse, as freshman Eric Murdock assumed the starting point guard role.

Among the humiliations experienced by the team during the 1987–1988 season was a moment that captured national attention during a 90-56 loss at the sixth-ranked University of Pittsburgh. The Panther's Jerome Lane shattered a backboard during a dunk. A photograph was taken as Carlton Screen scrambled to get away from the flying glass; the photograph was plastered in newspapers nationwide. (Courtesy University of Pittsburgh and Michael Drazdzinski.)

Athletic director John Marinatto and school president Fr. John Cunningham hired young, up-and-coming Rick Barnes to replace Gordie Chiesa. Barnes had only one season of experience as a head coach (George Mason University), but like Rick Pitino before him, he reinvigorated the college's program immediately. A superb recruiter, Barnes's bench coaching skills were often questioned during his six years at Providence.

Marty Conlon returned to the team to play for Barnes and the 1988–1989 Friars started the season by winning their first 13 games, the second-best season starting streak in the program's history. By early January, the team was 18th-ranked, but a 76-67 loss to Villanova on January 14 snapped the streak, and the Friars lost 11 of their final 16 games. Still, they finished 18-11 and made the NCAA Tournament. They lost to the University of Virginia 100-97 in the first round.

Carlton "Paco" Screen and Eric Murdock were known as the team's "men of steal." A disruptive defensive backcourt, Screen and Murdock combined to harass opposing guards for three seasons in the late 1980s. Murdock finished his career as the NCAA's all-time leader for steals with 376, while Screen chipped in 226 steals of his own, along with 1,076 points.

Marty Conlon was a 6-foot-10-inch forward from New York who flourished under Rick Barnes. Conlon was an outstanding passer and shooter, for a big man. He scored 1,135 points and contributed 584 rebounds during his career. Conlon's senior season was 1989–1990. The gangly forward averaged 14.7 points per game and helped lead the team to a second straight NCAA bid.

Throughout first 10 years of the Big East Conference, the one hurdle that the Friars could never overcome was to beat Syracuse University. The Friars were 0-21 in league play against the Orange. They turned things around when, on January 20, 1990, the team visited the Carrier Dome and raced back from a 10-point deficit to topple fifth-ranked Syracuse 87-86 on a last-second foul-line jumper by Eric Murdock.

The Friars continued their strong play by beating second-ranked Georgetown University 94-90 on February 13, 1990. The team earned another NCAA berth but fell to Ohio State 84-83 in overtime, after the Buckeyes hit a last-second three-point shot to send the game into an extra period. Still, the Friars finished 17-12, and the future looked bright with the nation's fourth-ranked recruiting class coming in.

Eric Murdock's senior season (1990–1991) was remarkable. Murdock was a virtual one-man show, averaging 25.6 points per game and capturing First-Team All-America honors. Eric scored over 40 points three times, including a Big East Conference record of 48 points against the University of Pittsburgh. He also scored 45 points against Arizona. Murdock, shown here with Marques Bragg (24) and Marvin Saddler, finished his career with 2,021 points, 504 rebounds, and 487 assists.

The 1990–1991 Friars finished 19-13 and earned a bid to the NIT. Junior Marques Bragg was a six-foot-eight-inch power forward who averaged 12.2 points per game and 8.8 rebounds per game. Seen dunking against West Virginia University in second-round action, Bragg finished his career with 921 points and 657 rebounds. The Friars edged James Madison University and beat the Mountaineers 85-79 before bowing to Oklahoma.

The 1991–1992 Friars were loaded in the front court but lacked shooters and point-guard play, finishing the season with a disappointing 14-17 record. Sophomore Dickey Simpkins anchored the middle and battled bigger opponents, such as Georgetown University's Dikembe Mutombo (35), in the Friars' January 6, 1992 loss to the Hoyas by a score of 70-63.

In the early years of the Big East Conference, Providence was overmatched up front, but by the 1991–1992 season, Rick Barnes had assembled the most physical front court the school had ever had. Center Dickey Simpkins (42) and forwards Michael Smith and Marques Bragg (24) gave the Friars the rebounding strength to compete against anyone in the league.

The team's highlight win during the dismal 1991–1992 season was a January 28 upset victory over 12th-ranked Syracuse University. In the 87-73 win, junior Tony Turner gave a preview of his outside-shooting prowess, which became evident the following season, when he nailed several long three-pointers to help upset the Orange.

Michael Brown was a six-foot-three-inch guard who played both the point and the off-guard slots during his career with the Friars. An unselfish defensive nightmare for opposing guards, Brown scored 1,163 points and had 359 assists in his career. As a freshman, Brown helped key an 81-66 upset win over 12th-ranked University of Arizona on December 22, 1992.

After struggling for two years without a pure point guard, the team's fortunes seemed on the upswing when Abdul Abdullah arrived from CCRI (Community College of Rhode Island). Abdullah could handle the ball like a magician, and although he was a poor shooter, he was a master at running the offense. In his two years with the program, during which the Friars had two 20-win seasons, he handed out 422 assists and had just 163 turnovers.

On March 12, 1993, Providence College squared off against the University of Connecticut in the first round of the Big East Conference Tournament. They came away with a 73-55 victory. Junior forward Troy Brown scored nine points as the Friars notched the 1,000th win of their history.

The Friars' heralded recruiting class of 1989 included Michael Smith, Dickey Simpkins, and Rob Phelps. In the 1992–1993 season, that class began to pay dividends as the team finished 20-13 and advanced to the NIT semifinals at Madison Square Garden, after beating James Madison University, West Virginia University, and Boston College in earlier rounds.

Dickey Simpkins was a 6-foot-10-inch center who anchored the middle for the Friars for four years. A superb defensive player, Simpkins scored 1,226 points and grabbed 790 rebounds but was often overshadowed by teammate Michael Smith. Simpkins helped the Friars to an 88-69 win over the University of South Carolina on December 31, 1993.

Power forward Michael Smith was the program's best rebounding forward ever. Smith pulled down 1,038 rebounds to go along with his 1,110 points. He was the only player to lead the Big East Conference in rebounding three straight years. Listed as six feet, eight inches but closer to six feet, six inches, Smith was a fierce rebounder. On January 25, 1994, he led the Friars to a 96-82 win over 13th-ranked Syracuse University with a league-record 26 rebounds.

The 1993–1994 Friars entered the Big East Conference Tournament 17-9 and, after beating Villanova, took on second-ranked Connecticut in the semifinals. Behind the scoring of Rob Phelps, who made 10 of his 11 shots, and tough defense by Dickey Simpkins on the University of Connecticut star Donyell Marshall, the Friars downed the Huskies 69-67 to advance to their first Big East Conference championship game.

Against Georgetown University in the Big East Conference finals, the Friars continued their hot play and jumped out to an early lead on the Hoyas. The team withstood several late charges to win their first Big East Conference championship 74-64 on March 13, 1994. Shown, from left to right, are Dickey Simpkins, Eric Williams, Michael Brown, Rob Phelps, and Abdul Abdullah (in-bounding the ball).

Big East Conference Tournament MVP Michael Smith cuts down the nets for the Friars. Smith scored 16 points, grabbed 16 rebounds, and registered a big late-game block against Georgetown in the Friars' title game win.

The Friars celebrated their championship on national television. Pictured, from left to right, are Eric Williams, Franklin Western, Dickey Simpkins, Abdul Abdullah, Troy Brown, Michael Brown, Pete Syzbilski, and Jason Murdock. Michael Smith peers in from below. The Friars gained an automatic NCAA berth but lost a first-round game to a tough Alabama squad 76-70.

The 1993–1994 Friars ended with a record of 20-10 (10-8 in the Big East Conference), and coach Rick Barnes departed for a job at Clemson after the season. Pictured, from left to right, are the following: (front row) Abdul Abdullah, Rob Phelps, Troy Brown, Dickey Simpkins, Michael Smith, Tom Hall, and Duffy McNulty; (back row) Michael Brown, Maciej Zielinski, Eric Williams, Austin Croshere, Piotr Szybilski, Franklin Western, and Jason Murdock.

When Rick Barnes departed, the college turned to Pete Gillen, an experienced coach who had spent nine seasons at Xavier University in Ohio. A brilliant game tactician, Gillen stayed with the Friars for four years and won 72 games.

Eric Williams co-captained the Friars in 1994–1995. A junior-college transfer, the six-foot-eight-inch Williams used a variety of spinning drives to the basket and outside shooting to score 1,001 points in just two seasons. With 27 points, Williams helped lead the Friars to an 85-81 win over the University of Pittsburgh on January 7, 1995.

The Friars began an unprecedented three-game winning streak over nationally-ranked teams by upsetting the fourth-ranked University of Connecticut 72-70 on February 27, 1995. Sophomore forward Austin Croshere chipped in six points and six rebounds to help down the Huskies. The six-foot-nine-inch Croshere would score 1,523 points and grab 645 rebounds in his career, while displaying a superb inside-outside game.

The Friars followed up their win over the University of Connecticut with a 71-70 upset over 11th-ranked Villanova on March 4, 1995. Austin Croshere and classmate guard Jason Murdock, Eric Murdock's cousin, teamed to reject the Wildcats' Jason Lawton.

The team's third consecutive win over a ranked opponent came in the Big East Conference Tournament with a 71-69 win over 20th-ranked Syracuse University on March 10, 1995, on two last-second Jason Murdock free throws. Michael Brown (seen here with the ball) chipped in with five assists. The Friars finished the season with a 17-13 record. They narrowly missed the NCAA Tournament and played into the second round of the NIT, losing to Virginia Tech.

The 1995–1996 season was one of near-misses and eventual heartbreak over missing out on an NCAA bid. God Shammgod was a six-foot freshman point guard whose ball-handling brilliance brought excitement to the Providence Civic Center as he assisted in a 58-57 win over the University of Wisconsin on December 11, 1995. Shammgod played two seasons with the Friars and then he left school early for the NBA draft.

After being left on the bubble with the NCAA Tournament, the Friars accepted a second straight NIT bid but performed poorly in an 82-62 drubbing by St. Joseph's. Shammgod led the team with 19 points, but the Friars' disappointing season ended with an 18-12 record.

Derrick "Flight" Brown was a six-foot-six-inch junior-college transfer whose leaping ability and outside shooting helped lead the Friars to the NCAA Tournament in 1996–1997. Brown scored 1,034 points in two seasons, averaged 17.4 points per game as a senior, and authored several big performances, including 31 points in a 62-47 win at the University of Connecticut. Brown scored 19 points in a 74-61 win over Columbia University on November 30, 1996.

One of the Friars' signature wins in the 1996–1997 season was a resounding 91-68 drubbing of eighth-ranked Villanova on January 6, 1997. Six-foot-nine-inch senior center Ruben Garces was mobbed by delirious fans after scoring 19 points to help Providence stop the Wildcats. The Friars finished the regular season with a league record of 10-8 and, after two wins in the Big East Conference Tournament, garnered an NCAA berth.

After opening NCAA play with a convincing 81-59 win over Marquette University, highlighted by Austin Croshere's 39 points, the team took on eighth-ranked Duke University. Derrick Brown scored 33 points, Croshere chipped in 21 points, and the Friars ran away from the Blue Devils in the last five minutes, which led them to a 98-87 victory on March 16, 1997.

In the 1997 Southeastern Regional finals, the Friars found themselves down by double digits to the University of Arizona with time running out. The team staged a furious comeback over the final few minutes, and this Jamel Thomas three-pointer knotted the score at 85 with 10 seconds to play. After a Wildcat turnover, the Friars set up for a final chance to win with 3.9 seconds left. Unfortunately, a Corey Wright three-pointer missed, and the team would lose 96-92 in overtime to the eventual national champions.

The 1996–1997 Friars ended with a 24-12 record and ranked 15th in the nation. They finished the regular season in a slump, but once in the NCAA Tournament, they went on a run that brought them within a jump shot of the Final Four. Pictured, from left to right, are the following: (front row) God Shammgod, Abdul Brown, Derrick Brown, Austin Croshere, Pete Gillen (head coach), Ruben Garces, Jason Murdock, Jamel Thomas, and Corey Wright; (back row) Greg Hamble, Kevin Keenan, Kevin Gorey, Mike Malone, Kendrick Moore, Mark Adams, Kofi Pointer, Ndongo N'Diaye, Llewellyn Cole, Rick Cordella, Dennis Cleary, Bobby Gonzales, Tom Herrion, and Alexis Sherrard.

With four starters gone from the Elite Eight squad, six-foot-six-inch forward Jamel Thomas was called upon to carry the load for the rebuilding Friars. An athletic leaper, Thomas scored 1,971 points in his career. Behind Jimmy Walker and Eric Murdock, he was the program's third highest scorer in history. He still holds school records for the most three-pointers and attempts. He would be the team's number-one scoring option in his final two years.

With no starter above six feet, seven inches tall, the Friars struggled in the 1997–1998 season. Erron Maxey, a six-foot-six-inch forward who filled in at center, emerged as a major contributor. Despite Maxey's efforts, the team was overmatched inside when playing the top teams in the Big East Conference. In a January 27, 1998 game against eighth-ranked University of Connecticut, the Friars were blown out 83-56.

Triumphs were few in the 1997–1998 season, but one came in a February 18, 1998 game against the University of Miami. John Linehan, Jamel Thomas, and Justin Farley celebrate a 59-57 Friar win. Thomas led the way with 21 points. The team finished with a 13-16 record, and Pete Gillen left to accept the head coach position at Virginia.

In March 1998, Providence College hired Tim Welsh, a dynamic young coach who had spent three seasons guiding Iona College to outstanding records. Welsh immediately took a team that was coming off a losing season and transformed it into a winner. On November 14, 1998, the Friars made their mark early in an 87-63 thrashing of 23rd-ranked Rhode Island, which was led by Lamar Odom.

Jamel Thomas had a sensational senior year for Welsh's Friars, averaging 22 points per game. Thomas's 22 points and five rebounds led the Friars to an 87-82 shocker over eighth-ranked Purdue University on December 27, 1998, with potential recruit Karim Shabazz in the house.

The 1998–1999 Friars finished with a 16-14 record and returned to the NIT, where they dropped a 92-86 shootout at North Carolina State, on March 10, 1999, despite Thomas's 25 points. The Friars had beaten the Wolfpack earlier in the season at home 80-69, but North Carolina State turned the tables on the Friars in Raleigh, North Carolina.

The 1999–2000 season was a disappointing one for the team—both on and off the court. Moments to remember were few and far between for a team that struggled without injured point guard John Linehan. One great moment occurred when seven-foot-two-inch center Karim Shabazz achieved a triple-double of 25 points, 15 rebounds, and 10 blocks in a 79-63 win over Long Island University on December 27, 1999.

The Friars slipped to 11-19 but pulled off a 61-60 overtime surprise over favored the University of Massachusetts on December 30, 1999. Karim Shabazz (3) had 14 points and 10 rebounds while Abdul Mills (11) made his presence felt. David Murray (40) had 14 points and dropped in a lay-up at the buzzer for the win.

Erron Maxey was a warrior for the Friars, a truly unselfish player who sacrificed for his team by playing out of position at center and power forward for most of his career. Throughout his career, Maxey scored 1,306 points and snared 738 rebounds. He led the team in scoring as a junior and senior.

The team battled back in the 2000–2001 season in a big way. The Friars rolled through December and grabbed an important win by topping 12th-ranked University of Connecticut 81-68 on January 13, 2001. Karim Shabazz and Erron Maxey each scored 12 points and helped to dominate the Huskies inside, as the hot-shooting Friars coasted to the win.

The Friars peaked with a stunning 103-79 win over 12th-ranked Georgetown University on February 10, 2001. The team set a Big East Conference record with 61 first-half points. They hit 14 of their 19 three-point shots and became the first team to score over 100 points against the Hoyas in league play. Karim Shabazz led the way with 22 points. Six players scored in double figures, and John Linehan handed out 10 assists. A week later, Providence moved into the Top 25 during the regular season for the first time since January 1989.

The Friars finished the regular season with 11 Big East Conference wins—the most in school history—and finished second in their division. They faced 14th-ranked Syracuse University in the Big East Conference Tournament and came up short 55-54 on March 8, 2001. Sophomore guard Abdul Mills averaged 10.9 points per game for the season and established himself as a future star for the Friars.

Providence faced upstart Penn State in the NCAA Tournament and was never quite in sync, losing to the Nittany Lions 79-69. Super defender John Linehan squared off against Big Ten scoring leader Joe Crispin and held Crispin to 13 points. Although the season ended disappointingly, the young and talented Friars turned their fortunes around with a 21-10 record.

Junior John Linehan returned from injury to lead the Friars to a successful season in 2000–2001 and was rewarded with the Big East Defensive Player of the Year Award, as well as Second Team All-Big East honors. Linehan entered his senior year with 246 steals—second on the Friars' all-time list—and 603 points.

The 2001–2002 Friars will celebrate the 75th season of basketball at the college. They enter the season with 1,143 wins and 724 losses. Shown, from left to right, are the following: (front row) Kevin Mahoney, Donell Allick, Rob Sanders, Abdul Mills, John Linehan, Romuald Augustin, Sheiku Kabba, Kareem Hayletts, and Tim Welsh (coach); (back row) Vince Cautero, Phil Seymore, Brian Schnurr, Leland Anderson, Chris Anrin, Ryan Gomes, Marcus Douthit, Garnett Thompson, Maris Laksa, Tuukka Kotti, Stephen Traugott, Steve DeMeo, and Bob Walsh.